THE ART OF

Cooking

with

Lavender

Washington Lavender Farm, Sequim, Washington

THE ART OF

Cooking
with
Lavender

80 RECIPES & 70 PHOTOS

Nancy Baggett

Copies of this book are available for purchase at: www.nancyslavenderplace.com

Published in 2016 by Kitchenlane Productions
P.O. Box 1453
Columbia, MD 21044

Photography: Nancy Baggett
Cover and Interior Design: Chrissy Kurpeski
Production Artist: Patty Holden
Copy Editor: Deri Reed

Printed in China

ISBN 978-0-9981836-1-9

The Lavender Connection, Sequim, Washington

Contents

Jardin du Soleil, Sequim, Washington

INTRODUCTION

I have cooked and baked my whole life, studied with a noted pastry chef, and, over the last three decades, have written 17 cookbooks. In the process I've accumulated lots of knowledge about how to make food taste good. But, of course, there's always more to learn. Since I came upon lavender, I find that I'm discovering new, exciting ways to make recipes more enticing nearly every day. I'm delighted to share with you the many tempting lavender lessons I've learned.

I had already grown and enthusiastically cooked with many of the familiar culinary herbs when I first encountered pots of bright purple-blue lavender at a garden center. I'd been reading up on this special herb and was primed to love it. Yet, its extraordinary fragrance and beauty still stunned me. Being well aware of the power of very aromatic herbs to make dull dishes shine, I couldn't wait to get started cooking with lavender. It was clear that a wonderful culinary journey lay ahead.

Very quickly I discovered that if you use the *right lavender,* and *with a light hand*, many, many dishes can be enhanced beyond your greatest expectations. No, they won't taste like the lavender in lotions and soaps smells. Cosmetics are normally scented with the (potent) essential oil of certain very pungent and resinous hybrid lavandin lavenders (*Lavandula* x *intermedia*), also sometimes popularly called "French" lavenders.

For culinary purposes, cooks need fresh or dried flower heads or buds, not lavender essential oil, which is too strong for cooking. One particularly sweet French, or lavandin, lavender 'Provence,' has long been been used for cooking. But there are other excellent, though less familiar, choices in the true, aka "English," (*Lavandula angustifolia*) family. (See more on choosing and buying culinary lavender on page 2.)

It turns out that culinary lavender is complex and has a really remarkable chameleon-like spicy, citrusy, piney character. It blends so perfectly with so many flavors and foods, it's often not even identifiable on its own. It just brightens, deepens, and enriches the taste of the dish it's in. I learned this simply by using crushed culinary lavender buds or lightly sweetened lavender syrup in all kinds of recipes and with all kinds of ingredients—from fruits, cheeses, vegetables, meats, and condiments to the dozens of other herbs and spices in my kitchen. An amazing number of the pairings (some totally unexpected) succeeded. Over time I realized that artfully cooking with lavender is mostly a matter of being aware of the synergistic combinations and flavor affinities and then taking full advantage of them. (See Appendix, page 120, for specific details on pairings and flavor affinities.)

At first, I experimented mostly with lavender in baking and sweet treats. Soon, I was completely hooked. Like vanilla, lavender just added a little something extra to nearly every pudding, cake, or cookie I tried. In sweets containing oranges, lemons, or honey, the something extra was huge! Today I absolutely *must* prepare my Lemon Pots de Crème (page 96), Peach-Lavender Freezer Jam (page 118), and (totally addictive) Candied Pecans (page 19) with lavender. Why would I leave it out when just a teaspoon or two can make a so-so recipe sublime?

Gradually, inspired by the positive results of my pairings as well as several recipes of innovative, influential chefs, I began to capitalize on the powerhouse potential of lavender in savory dishes. I riffed on a recipe of chef Larry Forgione featuring lavender, black peppercorns, and filet mignon to create my Beef Tenderloin Filets with Peppercorn-Lavender Sauce (page 58). The key elements were so good together, I teamed them up again in my more down-to-earth Cocktail Meatballs (page 10); these *always*

Purple Haze Lavender Farm, Sequim, Washington.

win raves! After loving a popular appetizer recipe of noted London chef Yotam Ottolenghi that featured creamy burrata cheese and blood oranges dressed with a lavender-infused oil, I successfully paired a fresh, smooth mozzarella in an everyday main dish salad with a lavender ranch-style dressing (page 41). I also included ham because I'd previously discovered from my taste testings that lavender and smoked meats, especially pork, adore one other!

I hope you're getting the idea that lavender can dazzle in all sorts of totally doable and irresistible dishes and are now ready to jump in. If you have culinary lavender ready and waiting in your garden that's great (see page 8 for guidance on growing lavender). But growing your own is not necessary: Depending on the season, it's often possible to buy fresh or dried lavender bunches or potted, organically grown plants at farmers' markets or garden centers. For a fun day outside, visit a pick-your-own lavender farm and enjoy wading into a sea of glorious purple and harvesting your personal supply.

Or just purchase a bottle or packet of dried culinary lavender, thumb through my photographs and recipes and choose a dish, and start taking your cooking and baking to a whole new level. Your recipes will taste fresher, brighter, and decidedly better, yet they won't take a lot of time or require any fancy chef skills. Turn the page and let's get going on this wonderful lavender adventure together.

Getting Started Cooking with Lavender

IT'S EASY TO GET COOKING WITH LAVENDER. Below are just a few basics on the kind of lavender to use, cooking methods, growing and harvesting, and general helpers and hacks to start you on your way. The recipes (all tested at least three times to ensure good results) are your roadmaps, so try to read through and familiarize yourself with the route before beginning a dish. Besides laying out the steps, all the recipes include useful introductory comments and the sort of practical tidbits I'd share if I were right there in your kitchen. I've also photographed a large share of the recipes to help you; the images show what the finished dishes look like, suggest serving and garnishing ideas, and, hopefully, inspire and entice you!

CHOOSING A LAVENDER FOR COOKING

Start the journey by making sure you're cooking with a *culinary lavender*. There are hundreds of varieties of this beautiful herb, and some are much tastier and pair with food much better than others.

You may have already heard of 'Provence,' and it is one "French" lavender that is sweet and mild enough for cooking. The other good culinary lavenders are the "English" lavenders, or *Lavandula angustifolias,* aka true, or common, lavenders. "English" means that they are hardy enough to be widely grown and available in the British Isles; like most other kinds, they originated around the Mediterranean. The *L. angustifolia* lavenders typically have a complex spicy, citrusy, piney character that adds a wonderful punch of flavor to all sorts of savory and sweet ingredients and dishes.

Culinary lavenders come in blues, purples, and pinks—there are really no right or wrong shades. (All those shown and listed on page 3 are culinary lavenders, and all are fine for cooking.)

Ironically, most of the more famous lavandin, or so-called "French," lavenders are actually pungent and resinous and not especially tasty. This isn't surprising considering that they are mostly grown for the cosmetics industry and their high essential oil yield, not for their culinary properties.

Some lavenders are ornamental plants only and are not edible. When buying fresh or dried lavender plants or bunches, avoid any labeled *L. stoechas* (sometimes called "Spanish" lavender)*;* these have distinctive cone-shaped spikes (the bloom heads) and little blossom topknots (as shown in the photograph). Likewise skip any *L. dentata,* aka *tooth-leafed* lavenders. These are too peppery and pungent to eat.

When buying dried lavender, be sure the product was harvested for cooking, not crafting purposes. Labels are not always helpful so in stores you may need to ask; sometimes you may surmise a lavender is edible simply because it's stocked with other culinary herbs! If you're shopping online, particularly look for descriptions like *culinary lavender,* or *Provence lavender*, *English or true lavender,* or *L. angustifolia,* or *L. angustifolia* blend. Some American lavender farmers package and sell individual *L. angustifolia* varieties: 'Folgate', 'Betty's Blue', 'Buena Vista', 'Melissa', and 'Hidcote Pink' varieties, and blends of them, are just some that

The *L. stoechas* (aka Spanish) lavenders are ornamental plants only and **are not edible**.

'Munstead'   'Cedar Blue'   'Royal Velvet'

'Provence'   'Melissa'   'Loddon Blue'

Here are just some of the many culinary lavenders to try. Lavender farmers often have their own favorites so ask for additional recommendations.

'Betty's Blue'	'French Fields'	'Irene Doyle'	'Purple Bouquet'
'Brabant Blue'	'Hidcote'	'Jean Davis'	'Royal Velvet'
'Buena Vista'	'Hidcote Pink'	'Melissa'	'Sharon Roberts'
'Coconut Ice'	'Hidcote Superior'	'Munstead'	'Sweet Romance'
'Folgate'	'Imperial Gem'	'Provence'	'Tucker's Early'

Lavender field at Jardin du Soleil, Sequim, Washington

pesticides, you'll be supporting sustainable, environmentally friendly family farming and agritourism.

EQUIPMENT AND TECHNIQUES

The Art of Cooking with Lavender mainly calls for the usual basic cooking equipment. You do need a grinding or chopping tool, such as a food processor, spice grinder, or coffee grinder (reserved for only grinding herbs), or a mortar and pestle. Like rosemary leaves, dried lavender buds are often too coarse and tough to be added to dishes "as is." Since it's unusual for dried lavender buds to come already ground or in their own grinder bottle, the first step is often to grind or chop them. (Fresh buds can be minced with a knife.)

A spice grinder (or a coffee grinder) is definitely the quickest option; pulse only a few seconds or the buds will be ground too fine. A mortar and pestle will do nicely if you enjoy preparing ingredients by hand. My preference is to use a food processor and grind ¼ to ½ cup of dried buds at once; I store the ground buds airtight and try to use them within four months. Depending on the processor, it takes 5 to 6 minutes to grind lavender buds to the right consistency—that is, ground into bits about as fine as dried thyme or oregano leaves, but *not* to a powder. The coarsely ground buds can then be measured out and stirred into dishes or sprinkled onto meats just like the more familiar culinary herbs.

You also need at least one sturdy, very fine mesh sieve; it's actually convenient to have both a large and a small one. Very often, lavender flavor is incorporated into recipes by steeping the dried or fresh herb in a liquid or crushing or grinding it into a dry ingredient. Once the mixture is infused with the

are especially aromatic and worth a try. Several of these and other culinary varieties are shown in the photos, and as you can see, each has a slightly different look (each has its own aroma and taste as well).

Much of the culinary lavender available in our gourmet and health food stores is imported, but if you're interested in the freshest product seek out local or American-grown. Many small, family-run lavender farms now operate across North America and often they sell their products both online and in welcoming on-site shops or barns. (See page 123 for more about online sources.) Consider visiting a nearby farm during the summer blooming season to buy what you need: The beauty and fragrance of the fields will take your breath away. And because lavender thrives with limited water and without flavor, a sieve is necessary to strain out the lavender buds or bits. Here are a few more helpful details on steeping and dry infusing.

Steeping

Lavender recipes often call for steeping fresh or dried buds in barely boiling water, but occasionally in melted butter, oil, cream, alcohol, syrup, honey, or other liquids. The method is particularly useful when buds or bits of the herb would detract from the appearance or texture of a dish. Once the lavender is strained out, infusions can be used immediately or, for convenience, refrigerated for several days. By the way, infusing melted butter and oil yields the fullest, most complex lavender flavor because fats most efficiently pick up and deliver the herb's key fat soluble aroma molecules to the smell receptors in the nose. (Remember, the taste buds can only detect components that dissolve in water.)

Lavender Wind Farm, Coupeville, Washington

Dry Infusion

Crushing, grinding, or mashing fresh or dried lavender buds into dry ingredients like sugar, flour, and salt using a food processor or mortar and pestle is another infusion method you'll see in these recipes. It's called for in making Lavender Sugar (page 110), and sometimes when preparing baked goods. The grinding action forces some of the essential lavender oil and other flavoring elements from fresh or dried buds into the dry ingredient. Directions then normally call for straining the mixture through a fine mesh sieve to remove any noticeable bits before adding the infused ingredient to the recipe.

Dried purple lavender infusing in hot water.

COOKING TIPS

Here's a grab bag of tips, hints, and hacks that will help you happily skip (or pleasantly meander) down the culinary lavender path.

- Fresh lavender spikes (the bloom heads) and dried lavender buds (technically known as *calyxes*) can usually be used interchangeably, but the fresh are slightly more potent and infuse mixtures more quickly.

- Avoid lengthy boiling of lavender or long exposure to high heat. Its fresh, pleasing citrus, floral, and herbal notes turn harsh and stale tasting as their volatile oils and other flavor elements break down.

- To extract lavender flavor by steeping, proceed exactly as for steeping tea: Bring the water *just to a boil*, then immediately pour it over fresh or dried lavender buds, or stir them into the water. Steep lavender tea about 2 to 4 minutes; for other infusions steep until the mixture cools or longer for a stronger flavor. Strain out the buds with a fine mesh sieve before using.

- Like rosemary, oregano, and cilantro, lavender is a potent, assertive herb, so when you begin cooking with it, use a light hand. (Some recipes suggest a quantity range, such as 1 to 1½ teaspoons, for this reason.) Once you're accustomed to (hooked on?) its distinctive, addictive character, you may want to add the larger amount.

- Try subbing lavender in recipes calling for rosemary or thyme. Lavender has a somewhat similar scent and pungency, yet is a nice change of pace, especially when paired with lamb, pork, smoked meats, duck, and other poultry.

- Don't let meats stand in a lavender marinade more than 24 hours. The flavor can become harsh and off-tasting.

Lavender drying at Deep Creek Lavender Farm, Accident, MD

- Along with its citrus and floral notes, lavender has some slightly bitter piney elements that need counterbalancing in certain savory dishes. Try adding a little honey, dried or fresh fruit, or fruit preserves to smooth the pungency and bring the floral characteristics to the fore. And note that lavender will add welcome zip and spiciness to all sorts of sweet and sour recipes, from chutneys and salad dressings to barbeque sauces and soy-brown sugar marinades.

- Some varieties of culinary lavender are milder than others. Feel free to use a little more or a little less depending on the pungency of what you have.

- Unlike many herbs, the dried lavender buds or fresh spikes (the bloom heads), and not the leaves, are generally used in cooking. (They contain most of the volatile oils and other aromatic components.) Some experts say the leaves of culinary lavender are edible, though less flavorful. Others say they should be avoided. I use them in limited quantity, mostly as garnishing sprigs for plates and drinks.

- Dried lavender buds, like many herbs, become stale with long storage. Your nose will know: If your supply smells musty-dusty or has no scent, replace it. If you happen to have a large quantity, it will keep longer if you stash it airtight in the freezer.

- Bloom or dried bud color doesn't suggest how a lavender will taste: Some extremely fragrant and flavorful *L. angustifolias*, 'Betty's Blue' and 'Buena Vista', are vibrant blue or purple. Some other excellent culinary varieties, 'Folgate' and 'Brabant Blue', have medium or light purple blooms. Several other fine culinary varieties, 'Melissa' and 'Hidcote Pink', are pale pink when fresh and drab gray-green when dried.

- Color *does* affect how a dish will look. An infusion of deep purple lavender buds in water will be pale purple to pinkish and look appealing in jelly or lavender syrup. Grayish-blue buds will yield an infusion that looks rather drab. But, drab, pale-colored buds can be the perfect choice in recipes such as white creamy sauces, ranch-style dressings, or lavender sugar, where dark flecks might detract.

HARVESTING AND DRYING

During the blooming season if you have a lavender patch you can enjoy cutting a few lavender spires with kitchen shears or a sharp paring knife as you need them. The spikes (bloom heads) are ready for harvesting when about the first third of the buds are open. To keep the plants tidy and not waste the stems (which can be strewn on the grill to lend an appealing smoky lavender scent), cut them down to below the first set of leaves. If planning to harvest and store a whole row or patch, be sure the plants are completely dry first; to minimize any chances of mildew choose a sunny day and wait until the dew evaporates.

Ready fresh lavender for cooking by snipping off the spikes, then rinsing and patting them dry. Either chop the whole spikes or pull off and chop just the tube-shaped little buds—your choice.

If desired, pluck off the tiny flower-like bloomlets (called *corollas*) from fresh lavender spikes for adding beautiful color and tempting little pings of flavor to dishes. You can also garnish cold or room-temperature beverages and plates with them. (Serve promptly as they gradually wilt.)

Whether you buy fresh or harvest your own, you can keep fresh lavender in water a day or two, but once cut it will soon start to dry out. Then, bunch it together with a rubber band and hang it upside down, using a hook or paperclip, until fully dry. Snip off spikes as you need them, or harvest the entire bunch by pulling off all the buds with your fingers. To keep dried hanging bunches dust-free and to catch falling buds, secure a larger paper bag around each bunch. Store loose buds airtight in a jar.

Save harvested and dried lavender stems to use as kabob skewers or to place on the fire while grilling meats and vegetables (for a pleasing smoky herb taste).

GROWING YOUR OWN LAVENDER

I was once assured by a culinary colleague from northern California that lavender grows like a weed. Maybe it does in Napa and Sonoma, but for most of us successfully raising lavender depends on providing the right growing conditions. If you'd like to try it yourself, keep in mind that lavender absolutely demands well-drained, light or sandy soil, and also craves full sun. It can't tolerate heavy, boggy soil or wet feet, as I discovered when a hurricane once left my front yard herb patch flooded for three days. Even the hardiest *L. angustifolia* varieties are threatened by sustained temperatures below -5 to -10 degrees F. Some kinds do tolerate heat and cold better than others, so ask local growers for advice on which to plant in your area.

To avoid our seasonal drainage issues and heavy clay soil, l now grow most of the lavender in my yard in light loamy-sandy soil in very large decorative polyurethane foam pots with extra-large drain holes. The thick, though lightweight, foam walls do a good job of insulating the plant roots from Maryland's winter cold and summer heat, and the pots don't crack from freezing. If your situation or climate is similar to mine, this approach might also work for you.

Several years ago, I also started 25 lavender plants in an ideal (sunny, airy, well-drained) spot on my son's property. They are beautiful and thriving, and other than requiring harvesting and pruning take very little care. Getting out and harvesting my gloriously colorful and fragrant lavender patch each summer is one of my most exciting and gratifying annual events! And I revel in using my crop in my cooking all year long. Put in a few plants in a suitable location, and this reward can also be yours.

Appetizers, Snacks & Beverages

Cocktail Meatballs 10

Sweet and Sour Lavender Sauce 12

Pan-Grilled Herbed Mushrooms 13

Grilled Sweet and Sour Shrimp and Pinapple
    Kebobs 15

Sun-Dried Tomato and Lavender Bruschetta
    Spread (or Dip) with Crostini 16

Marinated Cocktail Tomatoes with Lavender-Oregano
    Balsamic Vinaigrette 18

Caramelized Sugar and Spice Nuts 19

Zippy Orange-Ginger Chicken Wings 21

Lavender-Orange Frosted Popcorn 22

Easy Lavender Limeade or Lemonade 23

Strawberry-Banana-Lavender Smoothie 25

Quick Lavender-Raspberry Cooler or Party Punch 26

Lavender-Ginger-Lime Cooler 27

Lavender Kir Royale 28

Citrus-Fruit Sangria with Lavender 29

Fresh-Squeezed Lavender Lemonade 30

Cocktail Meatballs

Warning! These little meatballs are addictive to the point that people usually gather around the serving bowl and rapidly scarf them down. So, if you're entertaining a crowd, consider doubling the batch. For convenience, you may also want to make their lavender-infused sweet and sour sauce well ahead so it will be right on hand.

To keep the meatball preparations as fuss-free as possible, I call for baking them all at once in the oven rather than frying them in several batches in a skillet. They are lighter and less fatty this way, though still juicy and moist. Of course, it's partly the zippy sauce that makes them so succulent and irresistible!

Lavender Sweet and Sour Sauce (page 12)

¼ cup fine bread crumbs or panko crumbs

1 large egg, lightly beaten with a fork

1 teaspoon **each** finely crushed or coarsely ground dried lavender buds and dried thyme leaves

½ teaspoon onion salt or garlic salt

¼ teaspoon freshly ground black pepper

1 pound regular ground beef (do not use extra lean)

Preheat the oven to 375 degrees F. Line a very large rimmed baking sheet with foil. Spray the foil with nonstick spray.

In a medium bowl, whisk together ¼ cup of the sweet and sour sauce, the bread crumbs, egg, lavender, thyme, salt, and pepper until well blended. With a large sturdy spoon, mix in the beef until the mixture is evenly and thoroughly blended, or work it in with your hands. Divide the mixture in half. Shape each half into 18 to 20 (1-inch) meatballs, spacing them slightly apart on the baking sheet.

Bake the meatballs, turning after 6 minutes, then again after another 5 minutes. If necessary, continue baking several minutes more until lightly browned all over and a meatball in the middle of the pan tests done when checked in the center with a fork. Remove the meatballs with a slotted spoon to paper towels to blot off the excess fat. Use immediately or cover and refrigerate for up to 3 days.

About 30 minutes before serving time, combine the rest of the sauce and the cooked meatballs in a large saucepan over medium heat. Heat, gently stirring occasionally to prevent sticking, for 15 to 20 minutes, until the flavors have mingled and the meatballs are piping hot. Serve immediately with toothpicks or cocktail forks. Makes 36 to 40 (1-inch) meatballs, 10 appetizer servings.

Sweet and Sour Lavender Sauce

Lavender adds a subtle, yet highly seductive note to this zesty sauce—which gets compliments and recipe requests whenever I serve it. It's both versatile and extremely convenient. Keep it in the refrigerator for up to a week to ready the cocktail meatballs, or the grilled shrimp on page 15, or perhaps a quick cabbage or cauliflower stir-fry. Or brush some of the sauce over chicken breasts or pork chops as they go into the oven to effortlessly zip up what otherwise might be a ho-hum entrée.

2 tablespoons safflower, sunflower or canola oil

½ cup finely chopped onion

1¼ cups ketchup

⅓ cup lavender sugar, homemade (page 110) or store-bought; or granulated sugar

2½ tablespoons soy sauce, preferably reduced sodium

1 to 1½ teaspoons finely crushed or coarsely ground dried culinary lavender buds or finely minced fresh culinary lavender spikes (the bloom heads)

¼ to ½ teaspoon freshly ground black pepper, to taste

2 to 4 tablespoons apple cider vinegar, to taste

In a nonreactive 2-quart saucepan over medium heat, combine the oil and onion. Cook, stirring, until the onion is tender and just beginning to brown, about 4 minutes. Stir in the ketchup, sugar, soy sauce, lavender, and pepper. Gradually stir in the vinegar; taste and add more until the desired level of tartness is reached.

Adjust the heat so the mixture boils gently and cook, uncovered, stirring occasionally, until the flavors are well blended and the sauce is slightly thickened, about 6 minutes. Use immediately or refrigerate in a covered nonreactive container for up to a week. Makes 1¼ cups sauce.

Pan-Grilled Herbed Mushrooms

Keep a batch of my Lavender-Herb Compound Butter in the freezer or fridge, and you'll be able to make these very savory, meaty-tasting mushrooms in just a few minutes. They are ideal for serving with steak, as shown on page 59, or grilled chicken, or for setting out as a light yet satisfying vegetarian (and gluten-free) appetizer. If you're entertaining, you can make them ahead, and then re-warm in the oven at serving time.

3 tablespoons Lavender-Herb Compound Butter (page 66)

1 tablespoon fresh lemon juice, plus more if desired

½ teaspoon fine sea salt, plus more to taste

¼ teaspoon freshly ground black pepper, or more to taste

1½ pounds small (1-inch or similar) whole button mushrooms, cleaned and stems removed

About 1 teaspoon chopped chives for garnish

About 1 teaspoon finely chopped fresh lavender spikes (bloom heads) for garnish, optional

Heat the compound butter, lemon juice, salt, and pepper in a large (12- to 14-inch) deep-sided skillet over medium heat just until the butter melts. Remove the skillet from the burner. Thoroughly stir the mushrooms into the butter mixture. Let stand, stirring once or twice, for 5 to 10 minutes to marinate.

Return the skillet to high heat and cook, stirring and turning the mushrooms, until they are seared and cooked through and the liquid evaporates from the pan, 3 to 7 minutes depending on their size. As needed, adjust the heat so the mushrooms brown but don't burn. Stir in the chives, and the lavender (if using). Remove from the heat. Taste and add more salt and pepper or a squeeze or two of lemon juice, as desired.

Serve immediately in a serving bowl along with toothpicks for an appetizer, or with a large spoon for a side dish. Or serve the mushrooms as a garnish alongside steak or another beef dish. You can make the mushrooms up to two days ahead, then reheat in the oven before serving. Makes about 6 side dish or 8 appetizer servings.

Grilled Sweet and Sour
Shrimp and Pineapple Kebobs

These always disappear fast, and if you've readied the Sweet and Sour Lavender Sauce, page 12, the recipe goes together quickly. Bamboo skewers are fine, but if you have some sturdy dried lavender stems on hand, they will add a little smoky herb flavor, not to mention a little presentation pizzazz!

1½ pounds large (about 35) peeled, deveined fresh shrimp

1½ to 2 cups fresh pineapple cubes (¾-inch each)

½ cup 1-inch pieces sweet red pepper, optional

2 teaspoons chopped fresh cilantro leaves, optional

1 cup Sweet and Sour Lavender Sauce, page 12

Olive oil for brushing grill rack

Sea salt and freshly ground black pepper to taste

Soak 8 to 10 8-inch bamboo skewers or very sturdy lavender stems in water for about 30 minutes. Combine the shrimp, pineapple, sweet pepper pieces (if using), cilantro (if using) and sweet and sour sauce in a large, sturdy plastic bag. Add ⅔ cup sauce, close the bag tightly, then squeeze and shake until the shrimp are well coated. Refrigerate for 20 minutes. Then thread the shrimp, pineapple cubes, and sweet pepper pieces (if using) onto the skewers or stems, alternating the pieces for the most colorful appearance.

Generously brush a charcoal grill rack with olive oil using a basting brush or paper towels. Heat until the heat has reduced to medium and the flames have died down. Place the skewers on the grill about 4 to 6 inches from the coals. Cover and grill for 2 minutes, then turn them over and grill for 2 more minutes or until the shrimp are just pink and curled, but not burned. Sprinkle with a little salt and pepper, to taste, then serve the skewers with a bowl of the remaining ⅓ cup sauce to use for dipping. Makes 8 to 10 appetizer servings.

Sun-Dried Tomato and Lavender Bruschetta Spread (or Dip) with Crostini

Yes, it's possible to buy bruschetta spreads, but this one is so easy, healthful, and tasty, I never even consider serving store-bought anymore. This recipe demonstrates how lavender can work in concert with several other herbs to spark a savory dish. Snackers always dig in and eat a lot of the spread, so consider doubling the recipe. Those who have only tasted lavender in sweets are usually intrigued to find that it's just as appealing—but utterly different—in savory recipes.

Both the spread and the crostini slices can be readied well ahead, so this makes very convenient party fare—especially if you are hosting vegetarians. Simply set out the spread and crisp toasted bread slices, and perhaps shredded or fresh-grated Parmesan and diced tomatoes for garnish, and let your company fix their own appetizers. Another option: Skip the crostini and serve the mixture as a dip along with bread sticks or crisp pita chips, or assorted crudités for gluten-free guests.

½ cup extra-virgin olive oil

⅔ cup chopped drained oil-packed sun-dried tomatoes

1 cup canned chickpeas or white cannellini beans, rinsed and drained

2 tablespoons Mediterranean Lavender-Herb Seasoning Blend (page111), or see Tip (next page)

1 small garlic clove, chopped, optional

1 teaspoon granulated sugar, to taste, optional

Generous ¼ teaspoon **each** sea salt and black pepper, plus more as needed

1 (22- to 24-inch-long) French baguette loaf

½ cup shredded Parmesan cheese for garnish, optional

1 cup diced tomatoes for garnish, optional

To ready the spread: In a food processor, combine ¼ cup of the oil, the sun-dried tomatoes, chickpeas, 1½ tablespoons of the herb blend, and the garlic (if using). Process until the tomatoes are finely chopped and the spread is nearly smooth, 2 or 4 minutes; stop and scrape down the sides several times. Taste and add the sugar, salt, and pepper, as desired. Serve immediately or refrigerate, covered, for up to 2 days.

To ready the crostini: Preheat the oven to 350 degrees F. Line a large baking sheet with parchment.

Using a serrated knife, cut the baguette crosswise on a diagonal into ⅓-inch-thick slices. Stir together the remaining ¼ cup olive oil and the remaining ½ tablespoon herb blend. Brush the slices lightly on both sides with the seasoned olive oil, adding a very light sprinkling of salt and pepper to the tops, if desired. Place the slices on the baking sheet.

Bake for about 6 minutes on one side, then turn the slices over and bake until beginning to brown, 6 to 8 minutes longer. Serve immediately; or if preferred, let the crostini cool completely

Tip: If you don't have my Mediterranean Lavender-Herb Seasoning Blend on hand, make a quick mini-portion by stirring together 2 teaspoons **each** finely crushed or coarsely ground dried culinary lavender buds, dried thyme leaves, and dried oregano leaves.

and pack airtight in plastic bags and freeze for up to a week. At serving time, let the slices thaw at room temperature, then wrap in foil and warm a few minutes in a low oven.

To serve: Set out the sun-dried tomato spread, crostini slices, and the Parmesan and diced tomatoes if desired. Makes 5 or 6 appetizer servings.

Marinated Cocktail Tomatoes with Lavender-Oregano Balsamic Vinaigrette

So simple, yet so colorful and savory, these small lightly dressed tomatoes fit in nicely with an assortment of appetizers on a buffet table or tray, especially in summer when tomatoes are at their best. For a more substantial starter, include the mozzarella. Another possibility: Double the recipe and serve as a salad along with a meal.

3 tablespoons extra-virgin olive oil

1 tablespoon Lavender Aged Balsamic Vinegar (page 113), or substitute plain aged balsamic vinegar

1 tablespoon very finely chopped fresh chives or green onion, plus more for optional garnish

1 teaspoon finely minced fresh culinary lavender spikes (bloom heads) or finely crushed or coarsely ground dried culinary lavender buds

1 teaspoon finely chopped fresh oregano leaves or dried oregano leaves

½ teaspoon **each** finely minced fresh garlic and fine sea salt, plus more salt to taste

¼ teaspoon freshly ground black pepper

2½ cups small whole cocktail tomatoes, mixed colors if desired

1 cup ¾-inch cubes fresh mozzarella, optional

In a medium nonreactive bowl, thoroughly stir together the oil, vinegar, chives, lavender, oregano, garlic, salt, and pepper. Stir in the tomatoes until thoroughly coated with the vinaigrette. Right before serving, stir in the mozzarella, if using. Place in a serving bowl and add more salt if desired. Garnish with more chives, if desired. Serve with toothpicks or cocktail forks. Makes 5 or 6 appetizer servings.

Caramelized Sugar and Spice Nuts

"Simple, yet extraordinary" describes these can't-eat-just-one treats. Serve them as cocktail or party nibbles, or on a dessert, fruit, or cheese tray , or to garnish salads, as shown on page 43. You can also package them prettily for a fine holiday or hostess gift. I find caramelized pecans particularly addictive, but can't say no to walnuts or cashews fixed this way either!

You can salt the nuts lightly just to bring out their flavor, or for a noticeably salty-sweet taste, sprinkle with more sea salt as you remove them from the oven. Note that you'll need some lavender sugar to make this recipe.

¾ cup lavender sugar, homemade (page 110) or store-bought

¼ teaspoon fine flake sea salt, plus more if desired

Generous ¼ teaspoon **each** ground allspice and ground cinnamon

2 to 3 pinches ground cayenne pepper, optional

3 cups unsalted pecan, walnut, or cashew halves

Tip: If you happen to be out of the spices, it's fine to ready the nuts without them—they're good "plain," too!

Preheat the oven to 350 degrees F. Line a large rimmed baking sheet with heavy duty aluminum foil and set aside.

Using a wooden spoon, stir together the lavender sugar and salt in a 12-inch ovenproof skillet over medium-high heat. Stir constantly until the sugar starts to melt, usually in 2 minutes. Working carefully, continuously stir and scrape the sugar into a center pool until most is melted; take care not touch or splash it onto yourself as it is extremely hot.

Quickly stir the allspice, cinnamon, and cayenne (if using) into the melted sugar until blended. Then stir in the nuts until they are all coated, about 2 minutes. Don't worry if the coating isn't completely even. (If at any point the pan smokes or the sugar or nuts smell burned lift the pan from the burner, stirring.) Immediately transfer the skillet to the middle oven rack. Roast the nuts, stirring every 3 minutes, until nicely browned and fragrant but not burned, 7 to 9 minutes.

Remove the skillet from the oven using a pot holder. Immediately sprinkle over and stir in additional salt, if desired. Stir well, then spread the nuts out on the foil-lined pan. With table forks, separate any clumps or clusters; *don't touch* the nuts as they are extremely hot. Let cool completely. Break up any remaining clumps with your hands. Store, airtight, in a cool spot for several weeks, or refrigerate for up to a month. Serve at room temperature. Makes a generous 3½ cups candied nuts.

Zippy Orange-Ginger Chicken Wings

These Asian-style, spicy, tangy-sweet chicken wings are perfect for tailgating, or a picnic, or a Super Bowl party. They are marinated, then baked in a hot oven. They can then be served right away or stored and reheated, so are convenient for entertaining. If you wish, double the recipe; you'll need to bake the chicken in two batches.

Tip: Reserve the wing tips for making soup.

Generous ¾ cup **each** sweet (not Seville) orange marmalade and ketchup

3 to 4 tablespoons soy sauce, preferably reduced sodium, to taste

1 tablespoon **each** apple cider vinegar and Dijon mustard

1 tablespoon very finely crushed or coarsely ground dried culinary lavender buds

1 ½ teaspoons finely minced peeled fresh gingerroot

¼ to ½ teaspoon ground cayenne pepper, to taste

¼ teaspoon freshly ground black pepper

About 12 meaty (4-ounce) chicken wings (about 3 ½ pounds), tips removed and remaining parts separated

Thoroughly stir together the marmalade, ketchup, soy sauce, vinegar, mustard, lavender, gingerroot, cayenne, and black pepper in a bowl. Set aside ¾ cup to use as a sauce. Put the chicken pieces and the remainder of the mixture in large, sturdy 1-gallon plastic zip bag. Seal the bag, then shake it thoroughly until the pieces are all coated. Refrigerate at least 2 hours or up to 12 hours.

Preheat the oven to 375 degrees F. Set out a very large rimmed baking sheet and grease or spray with nonstick spray coating.

Thoroughly drain the marinated chicken in a colander. Transfer the drained chicken to a large bowl, then thoroughly stir together with about half the reserved sauce. Spread out the pieces in the baking sheet. Bake in the upper third of the oven for 20 minutes. Turn over the pieces and bake for 20 to 25 minutes longer, or until cooked through and nicely browned. Transfer the pieces with a slotted spoon to a heatproof serving dish. Thoroughly stir in the remaining sauce. Serve immediately or let cool, then cover and refrigerate for up to 3 days and rewarm in the oven before serving. Makes 24 chicken pieces, 6 to 8 appetizer servings.

Lavender-Orange Frosted Popcorn

Beware! This popcorn can be habit forming—especially if you're partial to crispy-crunchy-salty-smoky sweets. It's roughly inspired by our humble, old-fashioned Cracker Jacks, but here the corn is seasoned with a blend of lavender sugar, orange zest, salt, and smoked tea. The combo is on the gourmet end of the snack spectrum; nibblers who wouldn't touch the old-fashioned kids' favorite will scarf down this treat. But many kids love the popcorn as well.

In some dishes lavender comes across as herbal, but here it tastes a bit like nutmeg or allspice. People often ask what spice is used and look skeptical when I tell them the recipe includes **no** spices.

Tip: The lapsang souchong called for is a pinewood-smoked tea that adds a unique, pungent, natural smoke flavor. It may seem overpowering, but when the small amount mingles with other ingredients, it contributes a subtle, haunting flavor note. Look for lapsang souchong in well-stocked tea sections or tea shops, or order it online. (If you've got bagged rather than loose tea, simply tear open a packet and measure out what you need.) Even without this tea, the popcorn will still be addictive.

The recipe may be doubled. In this case, divide the popcorn in half and spread on two baking sheets.

⅓ cup plus 1 tablespoon granulated sugar

1 to 1½ teaspoons dried culinary lavender buds, to taste

1¼ teaspoons lapsang souchong tea leaves, optional

Generous ¼ teaspoon freshly grated orange zest

¼ teaspoon smoked sea salt or regular sea salt, or more to taste

1 large egg white, lightly beaten with a fork

10 cups lightly salted popped popcorn (do not use air-popped or flavored popcorn)

Preheat the oven to 300 degrees F. Line a very large rimmed baking sheet with aluminum foil.

Combine the sugar, lavender, tea leaves (if using), orange zest, and salt in a food processor. Process for 4 to 5 minutes until the lavender and tea are very finely ground. Add the egg white and process until evenly incorporated, about 1 minute, stopping and scraping down the sides once or twice.

Put the popcorn in a very large bowl; if freshly popped, let it cool completely. Pour the sugar mixture over top, stirring and turning until the kernels are evenly coated and the sugar is very evenly dispersed.

Turn out the popcorn onto the baking sheet, spreading to form an even layer. Bake in the middle third of the oven, stirring to redistribute several times, until crispy and dry, 15 to 20 minutes, or until just slightly darker. Set aside on a wire rack until completely cooled. Pack in tins or other airtight containers. Store for up to a 1 week, unrefrigerated; or for up to 2 weeks. Makes 6 (1½ cup) servings.

Easy Lavender Limeade or Lemonade

When temperatures soar, I fight back with quick, bracing pitchers of this lavender limeade or lemonade. Cans of frozen concentrate make it possible to avoid squeezing lots of limes or lemons, and still enjoy a treat with fresh citrus taste. Lavender limeade and lemonade are a huge hit with my family, and I'm guessing they will also be with yours.

½ cup water

1 tablespoon chopped fresh culinary lavender spikes (bloom heads) or dried culinary lavender buds

3 to 4 cups ice cubes, plus more if needed

1 12-ounce can frozen limeade concentrate or lemonade concentrate

5 or 6 lime or lemon slices or wedges for garnish

5 or 6 fresh lavender sprigs for garnish, optional

Bring the water just to a boil in a nonreactive container. Stir in the lavender, mashing it against the container sides several times. Set asid to steep for 10 to 15 minutes.

Just before serving, in a large pitcher, stir together the ice cubes, frozen limeade or lemonade concentrate, and 3 cans cold water (measured using the juice can). Strain the steeped lavender through a fine mesh sieve into the pitcher, pressing down with a spoon to extract as much water as possible. Stir well, adding more ice cubes as needed. Garnish with lime or lemon slices and lavender sprigs (if available). Makes 1½ quarts, about 6 (9-ounce) servings.

Strawberry-Banana-Lavender Smoothie

Lavender syrup or lavender sugar are always a convenient way to add sweetness and enticing fruit-spice flavor to dishes, so I suggest you keep them on hand. Here, either can provide just the right touch to a quick and tempting fruit smoothie. If you're usually rushing at breakfast or lunchtime, note that this drink can be ready in less than 5 minutes. And you'll have a nutritionally balanced meal: protein and calcium from the yogurt; vitamins C, A, and D and fiber from the fruits; and potassium from the banana.

> Tip: As bananas start to over-ripen in your kitchen, peel, divide each in half and cut into coarse slices. Seal each half in a small plastic bag and freeze. You'll be rescuing bananas that might otherwise go to waste, plus they'll be ready to pop into the blender or food processor.

1 (5.3-ounce) carton low-fat or nonfat plain Greek-style yogurt

1 cup coarsely sliced fresh or frozen (partially thawed) strawberries

½ medium-size fully ripe banana, cut into chunks

¼ cup orange juice or cold water

2 to 3 tablespoons lavender syrup (homemade, page 108, or store-bought) or lavender sugar (homemade, page 110, or store-bought), mixed with 2 tablespoons warm water

Strawberry halves for garnish, optional

Combine the yogurt, strawberries, banana chunks, orange juice (or water), and lavender syrup or lavender sugar-water mixture in a food processor or blender. Process or blend until completely smooth and well blended, stopping to redistribute the mixture and scrape down the sides several times. (A processor will likely take longer than a blender.) Pour into a large glass or two medium glasses. Garnish with strawberry halves, if desired. Serve immediately or refrigerate, covered, for up to several hours. Makes 1 (1½-cup) serving, or 2 (¾-cup) servings.

Quick Lavender-Raspberry Cooler or Party Punch

Depending on the event and your style of entertaining, you can make a very simple party cooler, or a slightly more elaborate, sweeter punch just by adding scoops of homemade or purchased sorbet. If you're in a rush, it's all right to use purchased ready-to-use lemon juice, though, of course, fresh tastes better. You do need some lavender syrup (you can make it, page 108, or buy it); I suggest always keeping a batch at the ready in the refrigerator. Double, triple, or even quadruple this punch recipe to accommodate a crowd.

1 quart well-chilled clear lemon- or lime-flavored soda, such as Sprite, Mist Twist, etc.

⅔ cup strained chilled lemon juice, preferably fresh

½ cup chilled lavender syrup, homemade (page 108) or store-bought, plus more if desired

⅓ to ½ cup fresh (or thawed frozen) raspberries

1½ to 2 cups ice cubes, plus more if needed

5 or 6 lemon slices for garnish

5 or 6 fresh lavender sprigs for garnish, optional

5 to 8 scoops Berry-Pomegranate Sorbet (page 100) or store-bought raspberry sorbet, optional

Just before serving, in a large pitcher or punch bowl, gently stir together the lemon soda, lemon juice, lavender syrup, raspberries, and ice cubes. Taste and add more lavender syrup if you'd like a sweeter punch. Garnish with lemon slices and lavender sprigs (if available). If desired, float several scoops of sorbet on top of the punch; as they melt, add a couple more scoops of sorbet. Makes 1½ quarts, about 8 (6-ounce) servings.

Lavender-Ginger-Lime Cooler

If you've never teamed up lavender with ginger and lime, be prepared for a spectacular treat. This zingy thirst-quencher is absolutely glorious for sipping and savoring on a sultry day. (You do need to have homemade or purchased lavender syrup on hand; my recipe is on page 108.)

Serve the cooler with or without rum—it's tempting either way. I sometimes skip the alcohol so the cooler can be offered to the children, but set out a bottle of rum so the grown-ups can spike their servings if they wish.

6 or 7 thin 1-inch round slices peeled fresh gingerroot

½ cup chilled strained fresh lime juice

2 to 3 cups ice cubes, as desired

½ to ⅔ cup light rum, optional

1 to 1½ quarts well-chilled ginger ale, to taste

⅓ to ½ cup lavender syrup, homemade (page 108) or store-bought, or Gourmet Lavender Fruit Syrup (page 109)

Lime slices and fresh lavender sprigs for garnish, optional

Tip: For the colorful layered look shown, serve the cooler without the syrup, then let everybody add and then stir in their own syrup as desired. The syrup color will vary depending on the fruit or berries used.

In a large pitcher, muddle and lightly mash the gingerroot with the lime juice. Let stand to infuse for 5 to 10 minutes. (Remove the ginger pieces, or leave them in for a more intense ginger taste.) Stir in the ice cubes and the rum (if using). Lightly stir in the ginger ale to taste. Add the lavender syrup. Garnish the pitcher with lime slices and lavender sprigs (if using) and serve immediately. Makes about 6 (9- to 10-ounce) servings.

Lavender Kir Royale

Kir is a classic French aperitif, usually made with a crème de cassis (black currant) syrup or liqueur topped off with a light, not too expensive white wine. It's sometimes prepared with a bubbly wine and is then called a Kir Royale. The sparkling version makes a simple but festive brunch or party aperitif.

I just had to see whether lavender syrup, or even better, my Gourmet Lavender-Fruit Syrup, could replace the usual black currant liqueur in a sparkling Kir. The answer is definitely yes! However, while trying out various flavors of my fruit-flavored lavender syrup with different white wines, I found that in addition to champagne, several Italian wines match up very well. Prosecco, in particular, has a great affinity for lavender-fruit blends. I think it's because Prosecco is made from very fruity Glera grapes, described as having notes of honeysuckle, fresh cream, apple, pear, and honeydew melon. Of course, lavender is often said to have these very same aroma notes!

Tip: For maximum pizzazz, use a couple different flavors of the Gourmet Lavender-Fruit Syrup when making these for a party. Then, as is shown in the photograph, garnish each glass with the same fruit that was used in the syrup. Guests just love this presentation!

½ to ⅔ cup well-chilled Gourmet Lavender-Fruit Syrup (page 109) or Lavender Syrup (homemade, page 108, or store-bought)

1 (750-ml) bottle well-chilled Champagne, Prosecco, Asti Spumanti, or other sparkling white wine

Fresh or dried long lavender sprigs or stems for garnish, optional

Fresh raspberries, orange slices, or other fruit for garnish, optional

Put 1 to 1½ tablespoons syrup in the bottom of 5 or 6 medium champagne flutes or other stemmed wine glasses. Top each glass with the wine, dividing it among them. If desired, thread lavender stems or sturdy sprigs with the same fruit used in the lavender syrup, and use to garnish the glasses. Serve immediately. Makes 5 or 6 (4½- to 5-ounce) servings.

Citrus-Fruit Sangria with Lavender

A light, colorful sangria is always a welcome warm weather treat, but this is one of the best versions I know. Most tasters can't identify the unique flavor, they just find it delightfully fruity and refreshing.

¾ cup bottled pomegranate juice

2½ tablespoons clover honey or other mild-flavored honey

2 to 4 teaspoons dried culinary lavender buds

¼ cup Triple Sec or peach schnapps

Strained juice of 1 small lemon and 1 small orange

2 cups ice cubes, plus more if desired

1 (750-ml) bottle light, fruity, white wine such as Riesling or Pinot Grigio

1½ cups well-chilled apple juice or sparkling apple cider

6 to 8 orange slices for garnish

Sprigs of fresh or dried culinary lavender for garnish, optional

Tip: If you'll be steeping the lavender in the pomegranate juice for only a half hour, use 4 teaspoons. If you have time to let the mixture stand and infuse in the refrigerator overnight, reduce the lavender buds by half, otherwise the lavender flavor will become too intense.

Combine the pomegranate juice and honey in a small non-reactive saucepan. Bring almost to a boil over medium heat, stirring until the honey dissolves. Remove from the heat; stir in the lavender, Triple Sec (or peach schnapps), lemon juice, and orange juice. Let stand to steep at least ½ hour, or cover and refrigerate, tasting for lavender flavor, for up to 12 hours.

Strain the pomegranate mixture through a fine mesh sieve into a large pitcher; press down to force through as much of the juice as possible. Stir in 2 cups ice, then the wine, apple juice, orange slices, and lavender sprigs (if using). Stir lightly, then serve immediately. Makes 1½ quarts, 8 (6-ounce) servings.

Fresh-Squeezed Lavender Lemonade

If you have never tried lavender before, treating yourself to a glass of fresh-squeezed lavender lemonade is a perfect place to start. It provides a great opportunity to experience how lavender tastes—it will probably be far more pleasing but also different than you expect. In fact, you may think it has somehow turned this lemonade into the best ever! I'm happy to tell you that lavender works the same magic in many other recipes, not just those with lemon!

Tip: The color of the lavender buds will determine the color of your lemonade. Vivid purple buds usually create an infusion with a noticeable purplish or amber hue; pale blue, pink, or grayish buds will produce only a faint blue or purple tinge. Whatever the shade, when the lemon juice is incorporated, its acidity will turn the lavender color pigments pinkish, resulting in a pale to bright naturally pink lemonade.

Generous 1 cup water

2 teaspoons chopped fresh culinary lavender spikes (bloom heads) or dried culinary lavender buds

¼ cup granulated sugar

⅓ cup strained fresh lemon juice, or more to taste

Fresh lemon slices or wedges for garnish

1½ cups ice cubes, or more as needed

Fresh lavender sprigs for garnish, optional

Bring the water just to a boil in a nonreactive container. Stir in the lavender and sugar until the sugar dissolves. Set aside to steep and cool for 10 to 15 minutes.

When the steeping mixture cools to room temperature, stir in the juice. The mixture can be used immediately, or for a more intense lavender flavor, cover and steep in the refrigerator for up to an hour. Taste it occasionally until the desired lavender flavor is obtained, then strain through a fine mesh sieve; press down to force through as much liquid as possible. Use immediately or refrigerate for up to 2 days.

At serving time fill two 10- to 12-ounce glasses with ice cubes. Pour the sieved mixture over the ice cubes, dividing between the two glasses. Stir until the ice cubes begin to melt and dilute the mixture to form lemonade. Taste and stir in a squeeze or two more juice, if desired. Garnish the glasses with lemon slices or wedges and fresh lavender (if available) and serve immediately. Makes 2 servings, about 10 ounces each.

Soups, Salads & Sides

Roasted Winter Tomato Soup with Lavender
Herb Blend 32

Zesty Mediterranean-Style Vegetable Soup 35

Chunky Herbed Potato-Corn Chowder with
Bacon 36

Fruited Chicken Salad 39

Ham and Mozzarella Pasta Salad 40

Creamy Lavender Ranch Dressing (or Dip) 41

Winter Citrus Salad with Orange-Lavender
Vinaigrette 43

Roasted Beet Salad with Thyme-Lavender Dressing
(or Roasted Beet Appetizer Bites) 44

Roasted Baby Potatoes with Lavender and
Rosemary 46

Variation: Roasted Cubed Sweet Potatoes
with Lavender 46

Lavender-Spice Winter Vegetable Medley 47

Roasted Red Onions with Honey-Lavender
Barbeque Sauce 49

Jeweled Rice Pilaf 50

Roasted Winter Tomato Soup
with Lavender Herb Blend

I love making this tomato soup in winter when I'm craving the flavors of summer but vine-ripened tomatoes can't be had. Roasting onions, garlic, and good-quality canned tomatoes concentrates and sweetens their flavor, and the lavender herb blend enriches their taste. Served with grilled cheese sandwiches, or perhaps crostini, this makes a heartwarming cold weather meal.

> Tip: If you haven't made up a batch of my Mediterranean Lavender Herb Seasoning Blend, substitute 1½ teaspoons **each** finely ground dried culinary lavender buds, dried thyme leaves, and dried oregano leaves.

1 medium onion, peeled and halved

1 large garlic clove, peeled

1½ tablespoons olive oil

2 (28-ounce) cans whole peeled tomatoes in puree

1½ tablespoons Mediterranean Lavender-Herb Seasoning Blend (page 111)

1 to 2 pinches hot red pepper flakes, optional

1½ tablespoons granulated sugar

⅓ to ½ cup light or heavy cream

Sea salt and freshly ground black pepper, to taste

4 slices or teaspoons Lavender Herb Compound Butter (page 66) for serving, optional

Preheat the oven to 400 degrees F. Spray a 9- by 13-inch glass baking dish with nonstick spray. (This helps keep the ingredients from burning onto the dish sides.) Add the onion and garlic, drizzle with the olive oil, and stir well. Thoroughly drain the tomatoes in a large sieve, reserving the puree. Add the drained tomatoes, lavender herb blend, and hot pepper flakes (if using) to the dish, stirring until well blended. Sprinkle the sugar over top.

Roast (middle rack), stirring two or three times, for 50 to 60 minutes, until the tomatoes have cooked down and thickened. Discard any onion pieces that look burned or dry. Scrape the tomato mixture into a blender or food processor and add the reserved tomato puree. Blend or process until completely smooth. (If the blender or processor is small, blend or process in two batches.)

Put the blended mixture in a medium nonreactive pot. Stir in the cream; use the larger amount for a thinner soup. Heat the soup to piping hot, but not boiling, stirring occasionally. Taste and add salt and pepper if needed. Serve immediately, topped with a round of lavender compound butter, if desired. Or cover and refrigerate for later use. The soup keeps for up to 5 days. Makes about 1 quart soup, 4 (1-cup) servings.

Zesty Mediterranean-Style Vegetable Soup

You may have heard that lavender is a classic in Provencal cooking, but this isn't quite true. Until the last half century the herb turned up only in medical concoctions, tisanes, and lozenges, and, rarely, in conserves. But now, regional cooks have begun using lavender, most notably in Herbes de Provence (page 115). Lavender is so good paired with oregano and thyme that I've created a Mediterranean Lavender Herb Blend and use it instead of the usual store-bought Italian seasoning mix. If you don't have my blend on hand, make what you need for this dish by combing 1 teaspoon **each** coarsely ground dried lavender buds, dried thyme, and dried oregano leaves.

Here, the herb trio contributes a distinctive savory appeal to this wholesome meal-in-a-bowl recipe. The soup is great for lunch or light supper, and is vegetarian if made with vegetable broth. The recipe calls for red lentils and quick-cooking brown rice, which reduces cooking time from the usual 40 minutes to about 25.

5 cups canned chicken broth or vegetable broth, preferably reduced-sodium

½ cup **each** coarsely chopped onion and chopped celery

½ cup **each** thinly sliced (crosswise) fresh carrots and 1-inch cut green bean pieces

¼ cup **each** uncooked red lentils and quick-cooking brown rice

3 tablespoons chopped fresh chives or trimmed and sliced green onions

1 tablespoon Mediterranean Lavender-Herb Blend (page 111)

1 to 3 pinches hot red pepper flakes, to taste

1 (14- to 15-ounce) can peeled, diced tomatoes, including juice

1 cup rinsed and drained canned cannellini beans, optional

2 to 3 tablespoons chopped fresh parsley leaves, preferably flat-leaf, plus more for garnish

Sea salt and freshly ground black pepper to taste

Stir together the broth, onion, celery, carrots, green beans, lentils, rice, chives, lavender herb blend, and hot pepper flakes in a 3-quart or similar pot. Cook over medium heat, stirring, until the broth boils. Reduce the heat so the soup barely boils. Cover and cook for 18 to 20 minutes, until the lentils and vegetables are barely tender.

Stir in the tomatoes, cannellini beans (if using), and parsley. Bring to a gentle boil and cook 5 minutes longer. If the soup is very thick, thin it with water as desired. Taste and add more salt, if desired. Serve in soup plates, garnished with more fresh parsley and black pepper, if desired. The soup may also be covered and refrigerated for up to 4 days; reheat over low heat, stirring occasionally. Makes 5 or 6 (1½-cup) main-dish servings.

Chunky Herbed Potato-Corn Chowder with Bacon

Mild and comforting, this home-style chowder is perfect for a cool-weather lunch or supper. The flavors of the bacon, potatoes, corn, lavender, and thyme mingle together for a very gratifying one-dish meal. Feel free to make the chowder ahead; its flavor actually improves during storage.

6 or 7 slices smoked bacon (don't use reduced-fat bacon or turkey bacon)

1 large onion **and** 1 large celery stalk, chopped

¾ teaspoon **each** coarsely ground dried culinary lavender buds and dried thyme leaves

3½ cups canned chicken broth, preferably reduced-sodium

2 cups peeled and cubed (⅓-inch) Yukon Gold, Red Bliss, or other boiling potatoes

¼ tsp **each** sea salt and black pepper, plus more to taste

1½ cups fresh corn kernels, or rinsed and drained frozen yellow corn kernels

1 cup light cream or whipping cream

Fry the bacon slices in a large skillet over medium-high heat, turning occasionally, until they are just cooked through and nicely browned. Transfer to paper towels to drain. Transfer 2½ tablespoons of the rendered bacon fat to a medium soup pot or saucepan; discard the rest. When the bacon is cool enough to handle, finely crumble into bits and set aside.

Over medium-high heat, stir the onion and celery into the bacon fat. Cook, stirring frequently, for 3 or 4 minutes, until the onion begins to soften. Stir in the lavender and thyme and cook, stirring, 1 minute longer. Immediately stir in the broth, potatoes, salt, and pepper. Bring to a boil over high heat. Reduce the heat to a gentle boil and cook, uncovered and stirring occasionally, for 12 to 15 minutes, until the potato is cooked through when tested with a fork.

If a slightly thicker soup is desired, working in the pot with a potato masher or the back of a large spoon, mash a few potato cubes. Stir in the crumbled bacon (reserve a little for garnish, if desired), corn, and cream and continue cooking, uncovered, for 5 to 8 minutes longer to reheat and allow the flavors to mingle. Taste and add more salt and pepper if needed. Thin the soup with a little hot water, if desired. Serve immediately, or cover and refrigerate for up to 3 days. Reheat over low heat, stirring frequently, to prevent burning. Garnish with bacon, if reserved. Makes 4 or 5 (1½ cup) main-dish servings.

Fruited Chicken Salad

Colorful and savory and livened with a light, creamy lavender-infused honey dressing, this chicken salad is perfect for serving at a luncheon, supper, or buffet—and ideal for entertaining because it is best made ahead. Diced celery and apples add crunch; dried cranberries lend chew and touches of sweetness; and all mingle to nicely complement the plump chunks of white meat chicken. Additionally, the salad is gluten-free and mild enough to please those with an aversion to spicy or exotic fare. Double or triple the recipe, if you like.

DRESSING

1¼ cups mayonnaise, preferably full-fat

1½ to 2½ tablespoons unflavored rice vinegar, white wine vinegar, or other mild, light-colored vinegar, to taste

2 tablespoons clover honey

3 tablespoons chopped fresh chives, or 1½ tablespoons dried chopped chives

1 teaspoon finely minced fresh culinary lavender buds, or ¾ teaspoon finely crushed or coarsely ground dried culinary lavender buds

¼ teaspoon **each** dry mustard powder, sea salt, and freshly ground black pepper, or to taste

CHICKEN SALAD

3½ to 4 cups ¾-inch-diced cooked chicken breast white meat*

1⅓ cups **each** ¼-inch-diced celery and ½-inch-diced unpeeled sweet-tart apples (preferably red-skinned)

¾ cup dried sweetened cranberries

4 to 6 cups mesclun or other mixed greens

Red and white Belgian endive leaves, for serving, optional

Fresh lavender blooms and/or chopped nuts, for serving, optional

For the dressing: In a nonreactive medium bowl, stir together the mayonnaise, 1 ½ tablespoons vinegar, the honey, chives, lavender, mustard, salt, and pepper until well blended. Taste and add a little more vinegar and salt and pepper as desired. Refrigerate for at least 30 minutes or up to 4 days. Stir well before using.

For the chicken salad: Combine the cooked chicken, celery, apples, and cranberries in a large nonreactive bowl. Add the dressing, tossing until evenly incorporated. Cover and refrigerate so the flavors can blend, at least 45 minutes or up to 2 days. Taste and add salt and pepper as needed, stirring well. Serve on a bed of greens garnished with the Belgian endive and fresh lavender blooms if desired. Makes 5 (1½-cup) servings.

* If not using previously roasted chicken breast meat, ready the chicken as follows: Trim all fat from 1 ½ pounds boneless, skinless chicken breast halves. Cut each breast half into 2 or 3 pieces. Place in a medium saucepan and barely cover with chicken broth. Bring to a gentle boil over medium-high heat, then lower the heat so the pot simmers gently. Cover and cook for 12 to 15 minutes, until the chicken pieces are just cooked through in the center. Test for doneness by cutting into the thickest part of several large pieces; if the meat looks opaque, they are done. Remove from the heat and let cool, then refrigerate, covered, until needed. Pat the chicken pieces dry with paper towels and cut the meat into ¾-inch pieces; use as directed in the recipe.

Ham and Mozzarella Pasta Salad with Creamy Lavender Ranch Dressing

Like many pasta salads, this one is great for making ahead and taking—to a block party, picnic, casual potluck, or similar warm-weather get-together. Since it features ham and cheese, it's more substantial than some pasta salads, so will also do nicely as a quick, ready-to-serve family main dish. The lavender-infused dressing mingles beautifully with the pasta, ham, and cheese; the dish actually improves with storage.

3½ cups cooked medium penne pasta or similar tube-shaped pasta, cooled

1 (8-ounce) ready-to-eat boneless smoked ham steak, well-trimmed and cut into ½-inch cubes

1 (8-ounce) package full-fat mozzarella, cut into ½-inch cubes

1 cup **each** diced celery and chopped cauliflower or broccoli florets

¼ cup finely diced sweet red pepper, optional

¾ to 1 cup Creamy Lavender Ranch Dressing (recipe follows), plus more as needed

1 to 1½ cups mixed red and yellow cherry tomatoes

2 cups crisp, torn romaine leaves and sweet pepper slices for garnish, optional

In a large nonreactive bowl, stir together the pasta, ham, mozzarella, celery, cauliflower, diced sweet pepper (if using), and the dressing and toss until well blended. Cover and refrigerate for at least 1 hour or up to 2 days, if desired.

At serving time, stir the salad well. Stir in the tomatoes and more dressing to taste if the pasta looks dry or the salad needs more zip. Serve the salad as is, garnished with sweet pepper slices. Or, line a serving bowl with romaine leaves, then fill the bowl with the salad and sweet pepper slices (if using). Makes 4 main-dish servings or 6 to 8 side-dish servings.

Creamy Lavender Ranch Dressing (or Dip)

This creamy-tangy ranch dressing was designed to go with the pasta salad on the previous page, but can also serve nicely as a dip for assorted vegetables or a dressing for tossed salads. The flavors mellow and meld during storage, so the dressing is best made ahead.

1 cup full-fat mayonnaise

¼ to ½ cup cultured regular or low-fat buttermilk, or more as desired

2 tablespoons finely chopped fresh chives, or 1 tablespoon dried chopped chives

½ teaspoon finely crushed or ground dried culinary lavender buds or minced fresh culinary lavender spikes (bloom heads)

¼ teaspoon garlic salt

Generous ¼ teaspoon **each** dried oregano leaves and dried thyme leaves

¼ teaspoon freshly ground black pepper

In a deep, medium, nonreactive bowl, thoroughly whisk together the mayonnaise, ¼ cup buttermilk, chives, lavender, garlic salt, oregano, thyme, and black pepper until well blended and smooth. If desired, whisk in more buttermilk for a thinner, pourable consistency. Refrigerate, covered, and let the flavors mingle for at least 30 to 40 minutes or preferably 1 hour before serving. Keeps, covered and refrigerated, for up to 1 week. Stir well before using. Makes about 1½ cups dressing or dip.

Winter Citrus Salad with Orange-Lavender Vinaigrette

The light vinaigrette beautifully dresses the simple winter citrus salad here, but do try it over a grapefruit, avocado, and escarole salad as well. Remember that olive oil stiffens in the refrigerator, so let the vinaigrette come to room temperature before serving. Also note that the color will depend greatly upon the oranges used: Some blood oranges are a deep orange-red while others are a purplish red. Regular juice oranges won't add much color, but their flavor will be fine.

VINAIGRETTE

½ cup extra-virgin olive oil

1 tablespoon chopped red onion

1 to 1¼ teaspoons chopped fresh **or** dried culinary lavender buds

5 tablespoons strained fresh blood orange juice (substitute orange juice if necessary)

¼ cup plain unseasoned rice vinegar

½ teaspoon lavender sugar, homemade (page 110) or store-bought, or plain granulated sugar

Scant ½ teaspoon **each** sea salt and dry mustard powder

⅛ to ¼ teaspoon coarsely ground white pepper, to taste (substitute black pepper if necessary)

WINTER CITRUS SALAD

3 to 4 cups mixed crisp bitter greens, such as escarole, romaine, curly endive, and radicchio

3 cups mixed citrus segments, such as oranges, blood oranges, tangelos, and mandarin oranges

½ to ⅔ cup Caramelized Sugar and Spice pecans (page 19)

Very thin red onion slices or shreds for garnish, optional

For the vinaigrette: Vigorously whisk together the olive oil, onion, and lavender in a small deep bowl. Let stand to infuse for 10 to 15 minutes. Meanwhile, in a jar with a nonreactive lid, thoroughly stir together the orange juice, vinegar, sugar, salt, mustard powder, and white pepper. Strain the oil through a fine mesh sieve into the jar, pressing down to force through as much oil as possible. Tightly cover the jar and shake well. Taste and add more salt, if desired. Shake well before serving. It will keep, refrigerated, for up to 10 days; bring back to room temperature before serving. Makes ¾ cup vinaigrette.

For the salad: At serving time, toss the greens lightly with 3 to 4 tablespoons vinaigrette. Arrange the greens in a salad bowl or divide among 4 salad plates. Arrange the citrus segments over the greens, then drizzle them lightly with more vinaigrette. Garnish with the caramelized pecans and red onion (if using), and serve immediately. If desired, pass the vinaigrette so diners can add more to taste. Makes 4 side-dish servings.

Roasted Beet Salad with Thyme-Lavender Dressing (or Roasted Beet Appetizer Bites)

You have a choice with this recipe: You can slice the roasted beets horizontally into rounds, then arrange them on greens and serve as a salad. Or create appetizer nibbles by cutting them into ¾-inch cubes and serving with toothpicks on an appetizer tray. Beets, thyme, and lavender are a dynamite combination, so either way the results will be extremely tempting.

> Tips: Walnut oil will add a subtle, earthy, pleasing note, though it isn't absolutely required. You do need homemade or store-bought lavender syrup though, so be sure it's on hand when beginning the recipe.

1½ pounds unpeeled whole beets, trimmed of tops and roots

6 tablespoons walnut oil or canola oil, divided

2 teaspoons finely chopped fresh thyme leaves (no stems) or dried thyme leaves, divided

1 teaspoon very finely chopped fresh lavender bloom heads or coarsely ground or minced dried culinary lavender buds

¼ to ½ teaspoon salt, or to taste

¼ cup apple cider vinegar

3 to 4 tablespoons Lavender Syrup, homemade (page 108) or store-bought, to taste

1 teaspoon smooth or grainy prepared Dijon or Dijon-style mustard

2 cups mesclun or other leafy mixed greens, optional

2 tablespoons crumbled very mild, creamy-rich goat cheese, such as Capricho de Cabra, optional

½ cup coarsely chopped walnuts, optional

1 to 2 tablespoons chopped fresh cilantro leaves for garnish

Preheat the oven to 400 degrees F. Cut any very large beets in half horizontally. Place them on a very large sheet of heavy-duty aluminum foil. Sprinkle over 1 tablespoon oil, 1 teaspoon thyme, ½ teaspoon lavender, and salt to taste. Stir briefly, then pull and fold the foil up around the beets so they are completely encased. Place on a small rimmed baking sheet and bake (middle rack) for 40 to 50 minutes, until tender when pierced with a fork. Set aside until cool enough to handle, then peel off and discard the skins. Cut the beets horizontally into ¼- to ⅓-inch slices, or into ¾-inch cubes if serving as an appetizer.

In a medium nonreactive bowl, thoroughly whisk together the remaining 5 tablespoons walnut oil, 1 teaspoon thyme, ½ teaspoon lavender, the vinegar, lavender syrup, mustard, and salt to taste. Add the beets and gently stir until coated. Cover and refrigerate for at least 1 hour, or up to 24 hours if desired.

To serve as a salad, arrange the greens on a serving plate or divide them among 4 salad plates. Arrange the beets on the greens, then drizzle over some of their juice. If desired, crumble the cheese over top, then sprinkle over the walnuts and cilantro and serve. To serve as an appetizer, put the beets in a serving bowl, garnish with the cilantro, and serve with toothpicks. Makes 4 side-dish servings, 6 to 8 appetizer servings.

Roasted Baby Potatoes with Lavender and Rosemary

Almost everybody likes potatoes—and now that the tiny, very sweet Yukon Gold potatoes are on the scene, roasted herbed potatoes are better, easier, and quicker to fix than ever. Here, lavender and rosemary team up with delectable, highly aromatic results. Serve with meats, poultry, or seafood, or as part of a vegetarian menu. Another option: Bite-size roasted potatoes are also well received as an appetizer (shown on page 45), especially if the Creamy Ranch Dip (page 41) is on hand to dunk them in!

Tips: You can substitute larger Yukon Gold potatoes if necessary; cut them into 1-inch cubes. Or substitute other golden potatoes if Yukon Golds can't be found. The same recipe can be used to ready cubed sweet potatoes; see the variation.

2 tablespoons olive oil

2 tablespoons unsalted butter, cut into chunks

1½ to 2 teaspoons finely minced fresh lavender spikes (bloom heads) or coarsely ground dried culinary lavender buds, to taste

1½ to 2 teaspoons finely minced fresh rosemary leaves or finely chopped dried rosemary leaves

½ teaspoon fine-flake smoked sea salt or regular sea salt

¼ to ½ teaspoon freshly ground black pepper, plus more to taste

2 pounds scrubbed unpeeled baby (1-inch-diameter) Yukon Gold potatoes

Preheat the oven to 400 degrees F. Combine the oil, butter, oil, lavender, rosemary, salt, and pepper in a 10- by 15-inch (or similar) low-rimmed baking pan. Place in the oven and heat until the butter melts. Remove from the oven and stir in the potatoes until coated all over. Spread them out over the pan.

Roast (middle rack), stirring occasionally, for 20 to 25 minutes, until the potatoes are lightly browned and tender when tested with a fork. Add more salt and pepper to taste. Serve immediately, or cover and refrigerate for up to 3 days. Reheat, covered, in a 325-degree oven for about 15 minutes. Makes 5 or 6 side-dish servings.

VARIATION ROASTED CUBED SWEET POTATOES: Proceed exactly as directed except used 2 pounds peeled, cubed sweet potatoes and omit the rosemary from the recipe.

Lavender-Spice Winter Vegetable Medley

This colorful, amazingly savory and fragrant vegetable medley will round out almost any dinner. It's an easy side to prepare while roasting poultry or meat, and is often a hit with those normally wary of vegetables. Of course, it's excellent as part of a vegetarian menu.

1 tablespoon unsalted butter

¾ teaspoon finely crushed or coarsely ground dried culinary lavender buds

½ teaspoon **each** ground coriander and curry powder

½ teaspoon finely minced peeled fresh gingerroot

½ teaspoon fine sea salt, or more to taste

2 tablespoons clover honey or other mild honey

1¼ cups baby carrots

1¼ cups 1-inch-diameter unpeeled whole baby golden potatoes or 1-inch cubes unpeeled baby golden or Red Bliss potatoes

1 cup ¾-inch-long and ⅓-inch-thick peeled parsnip lengths or ½-inch-cubed rutabaga

1 cup ¾-inch-cubed peeled sweet potato or winter squash

Freshly ground black pepper to taste

Preheat the oven to 400 degrees F. Combine the butter, lavender, coriander, curry powder, gingerroot, and salt in a 7- by 11-inch (or similar) glass baking dish. Place in the oven and heat until the butter melts and the spices are heated through, about 5 minutes. Remove from the oven and stir in the honey.

Thoroughly stir the carrots, potatoes, parsnips, and sweet potatoes into the honey-spice mixture. Roast (middle rack), stirring occasionally, for 35 to 45 minutes, until tender when a large carrot is pierced in the thickest part with a fork. Add more salt and fresh pepper to taste. Serve immediately, or cover and refrigerate for up to 3 days; reheat, covered, in a 325-degree oven for about 15 minutes. Makes 4 or 5 side-dish servings.

Roasted Red Onions with Honey-Lavender Barbeque Sauce

An easy, full-flavored side dish, these roasted onions go especially well with all sorts of roasted meats and poultry. If you keep a batch of my lavender barbeque sauce in the refrigerator, the recipe is a snap to make. Just stir everything together, slide in the oven, and bake alongside a roast.

Tip: You can slip some baby carrots in with the onions. Don't add potatoes though; the acid in the barbeque sauce will keep them from cooking properly.

3 or 4 medium to large red onions (about 2 pounds), peeled and trimmed

½ to ⅔ cup Honey-Lavender Barbeque Sauce (page 54), to taste

2 tablespoons olive oil or other vegetable oil

Sea salt and freshly ground black pepper, to taste

Preheat the oven to 375 degrees F. Spray a 2-quart (or similar) flat ovenproof casserole with nonstick spray. Cut the onions in half from top to bottom, then cut each vertically into 3 wedges. In a large bowl, stir together the onion wedges, barbeque sauce, oil, and salt and pepper until the onions are coated all over with the sauce. Spread them out evenly in the baking dish.

Bake on the middle rack, stirring once or twice, for 30 to 40 minutes. If the onions begin to burn on top, cover with foil the last few minutes of baking. Check for doneness by piercing several larger pieces in the thickest part with a fork; when just tender, they are done. Serve immediately or cover and refrigerate for up to 3 days, then reheat, covered, in a 300-degree oven. Makes 4 to 6 side-dish servings.

Jeweled Rice Pilaf

Roughly inspired by a classic Persian wedding dish called jeweled rice, this festive, fruit-studded pilaf works well as a side dish with lamb, pork, or poultry, or as a light vegetarian entrée. It needs to be prepared well ahead, so the flavors can mingle—which makes it very convenient for entertaining. Yes, the ingredient list is long, but notice that the directions involve only stirring all the ingredients together.

¼ cup safflower oil, canola oil, or other flavorless vegetable oil

5 tablespoons **each** clover honey and fresh lemon juice

1 ½ tablespoons soy sauce, preferably reduced-sodium

1 to 1 ½ tablespoons mild or medium curry powder, to taste

2 teaspoons finely grated fresh orange zest (orange part of the peel)

1½ teaspoons finely minced peeled fresh gingerroot

1 teaspoon finely crushed or coarsely ground dried culinary lavender buds

½ teaspoon ground cardamom or ground allspice

1 pinch finely crumbled saffron threads thoroughly mashed together with 1 teaspoon granulated sugar

½ teaspoon salt, or to taste

2 cups chopped celery

¼ cup chopped green onions or chives, plus 1 tablespoon for garnish

¾ cup **each** well-drained canned lightly sweetened mandarin oranges and dried sweetened cranberries

3 cups cooked and cooled long-grain white basmati rice (or substitute regular long-grain white rice)

⅔ cup pistachio halves for garnish

Fresh purple lavender bloomlets for garnish, optional

In a very large nonreactive ovenproof bowl, stir together the oil, honey, lemon juice, soy sauce, curry powder, orange zest, gingerroot, lavender, cardamom, saffron-sugar mixture, and salt until well blended. Thoroughly stir in the celery, green onions, mandarin oranges, and cranberries until evenly incorporated. Stir in the rice until coated with the seasoning mixture. Taste and add more curry powder and salt, if desired. Cover and refrigerate for at least 45 minutes or up to 24 hours.

To serve, heat the pilaf, covered, in a low oven, stirring occasionally until warmed through, about 20 minutes. Transfer the pilaf to a serving bowl or plate. Garnish with the pistachios, green onions, and fresh lavender bloomlets (if available). Makes 7 or 8 side-dish servings.

Tip: Saffron is extremely pricy, so if you don't have it and don't wish to purchase it, you can substitute ⅛ teaspoon ground turmeric with acceptable results. Turmeric will tint the rice yellow just like saffron, but it lacks saffron's rich, exotic flavor, so will not deliver the same distinctive and alluring taste results.

Meat, Poultry & Seafood

Beef Pot Roast and Vegetables with Honey-
Lavender Barbeque Sauce 53

Honey-Lavender Barbeque Sauce 54

Ham Fried Rice with Lavender 55

South of France-Style Spicy Fish Stew 57

Beef Tenderloin with Gourmet Peppercorn-Lavender
Pan Sauce 58

Pork Chops and Apples with Lavender and
Thyme 60

Easy Italian Sausage, Vegetable, and White
Bean Stew 63

Herbed Whole Roast Chicken 64

Lavender-Herb Compound Butter 66

Ginger-Lavender Grilled (or Broiled) Salmon 67

Lavender-Ginger Chicken Curry 69

Turkey Scaloppini with Lemon and Mediterranean
Herbs 70

Beef Pot Roast and Vegetables with Honey-Lavender Barbeque Sauce

A good pot roast is always a welcome cold weather meal and this one is both extremely succulent and full-flavored. The tangy-sweet barbeque sauce tenderizes and adds zest to the beef and, once added to the vegetables, zips them up, too. (Don't try to roast the vegetables in the barbeque sauce; its acidity will keep the potatoes from cooking properly.)

Note that you'll need to have a batch of the Honey-Lavender Barbeque Sauce on hand to make the pot roast.

3¼- to 3½-pound boneless beef chuck roast, trimmed of excess fat

Salt and freshly ground black pepper, to taste

2 tablespoons unbleached all-purpose flour

About 5 tablespoons olive oil or other vegetable oil, divided

2 cups canned beef broth, preferably low-sodium

2 cups Honey-Lavender Barbeque Sauce (recipe follows), divided

1 teaspoon crushed or finely ground dried culinary lavender buds

12 cups 1¼-inch chunks or lengths mixed vegetables, such as unpeeled Red Bliss potatoes, carrots, onions, turnips, rutabaga, parsnips, and celery

Tip: If the pot roast and pan of vegetables don't fit on the same oven rack, it's fine to stagger the veggies on a rack just below the Dutch oven.

Preheat the oven to 375 degrees F. Pat the roast dry with paper towels. Season with salt and pepper, and lightly pat all over with the flour. In a 6-quart Dutch oven or similar very large heavy ovenproof pot over medium-high heat, heat 3 tablespoons of the oil until hot but not smoking. Add the beef and sear, turning several times, until well browned all over, about 10 minutes. Add a little more oil if necessary to prevent burning.

Stir the beef broth, 1 cup barbeque sauce, and the lavender into the Dutch oven. Bring to a boil over high heat. Cover tightly. Transfer the pot to the oven (middle rack) and roast for 2½ to 3 hours, until the beef is tender when pierced in the thickest part with a fork; check occasionally, and if at any point the liquid reduces to less than about 2 cups, add about ½ cup of water.

Meanwhile, thoroughly stir together the vegetables, remaining 2 tablespoons oil, and salt and pepper to taste on a very large rimmed sheet pan or in a very shallow roasting pan. Roast, stirring occasionally, for 50 to 60 minutes, until the vegetables are just tender in the center when tested with a fork. Stir ½ cup of the remaining barbeque sauce into the vegetables until they are well coated; set them aside.

When the pot roast is done, arrange it and the vegetables in a large, deep, heatproof serving dish or platter. Cover with foil and return to the turned-off oven to stay warm. Return the

Dutch oven to the burner over medium-high heat. Stir in the remaining ½ cup barbeque sauce. Cook briskly, uncovered, until the liquid reduces to about 2 cups. Place the sauce in a 2-cup measure; let stand until the fat rises to the surface. Skim or pour off the fat. Drizzle half the sauce over the beef and vegetables. Serve the remaining sauce at the table so diners can add more to their liking. The dish is excellent made ahead and reheated in a 325-degree F oven. It will keep, refrigerated, for up to 4 days. Makes 5 or 6 main-dish servings.

Honey-Lavender Barbeque Sauce

I do hope you'll try this recipe! If you were thinking that commercial barbeque sauces are good enough and wondering if homemade is worth the effort, I assure you that in this case it is. Everybody who tastes this sauce—whether on the beef pot roast on the previous page or with the roasted red onions on page 49, or on roasted chicken pieces or grilled pork chops—swoons and demands the recipe. And, good news, the sauce is fairly simple and keeps well in the refrigerator. I find myself reaching for it to add zip to plain meat, poultry, seafood, and vegetable dishes all the time, so I often double the recipe. You might want to, as well.

1 cup **each** clover honey and apple cider vinegar

⅔ cup packed light or dark brown sugar

1 (16-ounce) can tomato sauce

¼ cup Worcestershire sauce

3 tablespoons safflower oil or other flavorless vegetable oil

1 tablespoon coarsely ground dried culinary lavender buds or finely minced fresh culinary lavender spikes

2½ teaspoons ground allspice

2 teaspoons **each** dried thyme leaves and ground ginger

½ teaspoon **each** smoked sea salt (or regular sea salt) and freshly ground black pepper

In a large nonreactive saucepan, stir together the honey, vinegar, brown sugar, tomato sauce, Worcestershire sauce, oil, lavender, allspice, thyme, ginger, salt, and pepper. Place over medium heat and cook, stirring, until just boiling. Adjust the heat so the mixture boils gently. Cook, uncovered, stirring occasionally, until the flavors are well blended and the sauce is slightly thickened, 6 to 8 minutes. Use immediately or cover and refrigerate in a jar or other nonreactive storage container for up to 3 weeks. Makes about 2½ cups sauce.

Ham Fried Rice with Lavender

If you're new to cooking with lavender, this is a good recipe to begin with because it shows off the unique flavor of lavender in a savory dish. A little reminiscent of rosemary or thyme, but not quite like either, its herbal character enhances all sorts of fresh and smoked pork dishes, including this fried rice and the hearty sausage stew (page 63) and pork chops with apples (page 60).

This simple recipe works well as either a quick side or entrée; use the larger quantity of ham suggested for a main dish. The recipe originally appeared in my story on how to cook with lavender for the *Washington Post*; I've slightly updated it here.

2 tablespoons safflower oil, sesame oil, or other vegetable oil

¾ cup coarsely sliced (crosswise) green onion, including tender tops, plus 2 tablespoons for garnish

¾ cup **each** chopped celery and red or yellow (or both) bell pepper

½ cup fresh or thawed frozen green peas, optional

1 to 1¼ teaspoons finely minced fresh culinary lavender bloom heads or coarsely ground dried culinary lavender buds, or more to taste

1½ teaspoons minced or grated peeled fresh gingerroot

1 to 1½ cups coarsely cubed well-trimmed thick-sliced baked ham or pre-cooked ham steak

2½ cups cooled cooked long-grain white or brown rice

½ cup golden or dark seedless raisins or a combination

2½ to 3½ tablespoons reduced-sodium soy sauce, to taste

¼ teaspoon freshly ground black pepper

3 tablespoons chopped salted peanuts or cashews for garnish, optional

In a 12-inch skillet, heat the oil over medium-high until almost hot. Stir in the green onions, celery, bell pepper, peas (if using), lavender, ginger, and ham and cook, stirring frequently, until the greens onions are softened slightly, 2 to 3 minutes. Thoroughly stir in the rice, raisins, soy sauce and pepper. Continue cooking, stirring, for 3 to 4 minutes, until the ingredients are well blended and the rice is heated through. Transfer to a serving bowl. Garnish with green onions and peanuts and serve. Makes 3 main-dish servings, 4 or 5 side-dish servings.

South of France-Style Spicy Fish Stew

I wouldn't dream of calling this bouillabaisse, or even hint that the recipe is an authentic Provençal fish stew. It doesn't include the local fish of the region or feature a fish stock, and, it calls for potatoes, which would doubtless raise a few purists' eyebrows. But this piquant one-pot meal does capture the spirit and robustness of the classic dish, and it shows off to great advantage the aroma and flavor of lavender and some of the other Mediterranean herbs. The stew will be improved if you use the optional saffron, but is still well worth making without it.

3 tablespoons olive oil

1 cup **each** diced onions, celery, and red or green bell pepper

¾ teaspoon **each** coarsely ground dried culinary lavender buds and dried thyme leaves

½ teaspoon **each** dried oregano leaves and finely crushed fennel seeds

¼ teaspoon **each** freshly ground black pepper and ground cayenne pepper

1 large garlic clove, minced

2 cups ⅓-inch-diced peeled thin-skinned boiling potatoes

3 to 3½ cups canned chicken broth, preferably reduced-sodium

Generous pinch finely crumbled or crushed saffron threads (optional)

1 (14- to 15-ounce) can diced tomatoes, including juice

⅓ cup chopped fresh parsley, plus more for garnish

1½ pounds boneless, skinless cod, haddock, halibut, sea bass, or other mild, firm white fish fillets, cut into 2-inch chunks

Fine flake sea salt to taste

In a very large saucepan or soup pot over medium-high heat, stir together the oil, onion, celery, bell pepper, lavender, thyme, oregano, fennel seeds, black pepper, and cayenne pepper. Cook, stirring frequently, until the onions are just beginning to brown, about 5 minutes. Stir in the garlic and potatoes and cook, stirring, 1 minute longer.

Stir 3 cups broth and the saffron (if using) into the pot. Bring to a gentle boil; cook, uncovered, for 15 to 20 minutes, until the potatoes are tender when tested with a fork. Add the tomatoes and parsley; cook 5 minutes longer. Stir in the fish and cook, gently stirring several times, until the pieces are just opaque and cooked through, 3 to 4 minutes. Thin the stew with more broth as needed. Add salt and more pepper or cayenne pepper to taste. Serve piping hot in soup plates, garnished with chopped fresh parsley. Makes 5 or 6 main-dish servings, about 2 cups each.

Beef Tenderloin Filets with Gourmet Peppercorn-Lavender Pan Sauce

Consider preparing this elegant but very doable recipe when you'd like to treat yourself or guests to a special meal. While rich and gratifying, it does have a slight piquancy that may not suit very timid eaters.

Be sure to use a "gourmet" peppercorn blend with black, white, green, and pink peppercorns. Some brands omit the pink peppercorns, but they are important here because they have a rose-like aroma that brings out the rose and other floral notes in the lavender.

1¼ to 1½ pounds (untrimmed) well-marbled beef tenderloin

1½ teaspoons freshly ground gourmet 4-peppercorn blend

1 teaspoon coarsely ground dried culinary lavender buds or finely chopped fresh culinary lavender spikes (bloom heads)

½ teaspoon dried thyme leaves

Scant ½ teaspoon sea salt or to taste

2 tablespoons olive oil, divided

⅔ cup reduced-sodium beef broth, divided

Generous ¼ teaspoon finely crushed fennel seeds

1 tablespoon unsalted butter

Fresh lavender sprigs for garnish, optional

Tip: The filets go nicely with the Pan-Grilled Marinated Mushroom, page 13.

Trim the excess fat and silver skin from the tenderloin, reserving all the scraps. Cut it crosswise into four filets and pat dry on both sides with paper towels. For the seasoning mix, stir together the ground peppercorns, lavender, thyme, and sea salt. For the marinade, combine 2 teaspoons seasoning mix with 1 tablespoon of the olive oil and 3 tablespoon of the beef broth in a flat glass dish large enough to hold the filets. Place the filets in the dish, turning until lightly coated all over with the marinade. Set aside to marinate for at least 15 and preferably 20 minutes.

Meanwhile for the beef stock, combine the reserved beef scraps, remaining beef broth, remainder of the seasoning mix, and the fennel seeds in a small saucepan. Simmer over medium heat until the stock reduces to a generous ⅓ cup. Turn off the heat and let stand a few minutes so the flavors can mingle. Strain it through a fine mesh sieve and reserve.

Pat the filets dry with paper towels. Heat the remaining 1 tablespoon olive oil in a 10- to 11-inch skillet over high heat. When hot but not smoking, add the filets and sear well on both sides, about 3 minutes per side. Add 2 tablespoons of the stock and continue searing until the filets are cooked as desired, 2 to 3 minutes for rare or longer for well done. (Add 1 to 2 tablespoons more stock if needed to prevent burning.) Cut into the meat in the thickest part to check for the desired doneness. Transfer the filets to a heated serving platter or individual dinner plates. Add the remaining stock and butter to the skillet; raise the heat and cook, stirring, just until butter melts. Taste and add salt, if desired. Spoon a little sauce over the filets; add to taste as it is quite piquant and pungent. Garnish platter or plates with a sprig of lavender (if using), and serve immediately. Makes 4 main-dish servings.

Pork Chops and Apples with Lavender and Thyme

Surprisingly simple but wonderfully savory, this makes a fine autumn or winter entrée and side combination. Roasted acorn squash or baked sweet potatoes are a good seasonal choice to round out the meal. If you've not paired lavender and thyme before, you'll find that they have a great affinity for one another, as well as for both pork and apples. This recipe is a supper standby at my house, though it seems fancy enough to serve to company.

4 (5- to 6-ounce) trimmed boneless center cut loin pork chops

2 teaspoons **each** dried thyme leaves and finely crushed or minced dried culinary lavender buds

Sea salt and coarsely ground fresh black pepper to taste

1½ tablespoons olive oil or other preferred vegetable oil

About ½ cup sweet apple cider or apple juice, divided

3 to 4 medium (peeled or unpeeled) sweet-tart apples, such as Braeburn, Honeycrisp, Golden Delicious, or Empire, each cored and cut into 6 to 8 wedges

Working on wax paper or other work surface, lay out the chops and sprinkle ¼ teaspoon **each** thyme and lavender on each side of all four. Lightly press the herbs into the meat surface with fingertips. Salt and pepper the chops to taste on both sides.

In a 12- to 13-inch or larger deep-sided nonstick skillet, heat the oil over medium-high heat until hot but not smoking. Add the pork chops and cook, turning about every 2 minutes, until very nicely browned on both sides, about 6 to 9 minutes. Add 3 tablespoons apple cider, stirring in until incorporated. Place the apple slices all around the chops, spooning a little more cider over them. Adjust the heat so the chops and apples cook briskly but don't burn, stirring the apples and turning the chops frequently. Watch carefully and as soon as the liquid starts to boil down, about 2 minutes, add 2 tablespoons more cider and continue cooking. When the chops are cooked through, 3 to 6 minutes longer, transfer them to a serving dish or platter.

Add 3 or 4 tablespoons more cider to the skillet and bring the heat to high. Reduce the cider and cook the apples until tender, stirring, until slightly thickened and saucy, then spoon the apples and pan sauce over the chops and serve immediately. (For convenience, the dish can be readied ahead, then reheated, covered, in a 300-degree F oven.) Makes 4 main-dish servings.

Easy Italian Sausage, Vegetable, and White Bean Stew

Unlike many stews and one-pot dinners, this one cooks quickly. In fact, once you start browning the sausage, you can have this humble, Mediterranean-inspired dish on the table in about 30 minutes. The assertive taste and aroma of lavender and oregano complement the flavor of the sausage and also brighten up the mild white beans. Add a loaf of crusty bread, or perhaps a green salad, for a satisfying meal.

1 pound mild Italian sausage in casings, cut crosswise into ⅓-inch-thick slices

1 medium onion, chopped

1 large celery stalk, cut crosswise into ½-inch pieces

1 large green or red bell pepper, seeded and cut into 1-inch chunks

3 medium carrots, peeled and cut crosswise into 1-inch-thick slices

1 garlic clove, minced

1 cup fat-free reduced-sodium chicken broth or regular chicken broth

1 (15-ounce) can white cannellini beans, rinsed and drained

1 teaspoon **each** coarsely ground dried culinary lavender buds and dried oregano leaves

Pinch of hot red pepper flakes, optional

1 (8-ounce) can reduced-sodium tomato sauce or regular tomato sauce

⅛ to ¼ teaspoon **each** sea salt and black pepper, or to taste

Chopped fresh parsley for garnish, optional

In a 4-quart or larger heavy saucepan or similar pot, sear the sausage over high heat, turning frequently, until well browned on all sides, about 10 minutes. Add the onion, celery, bell pepper, carrots, and garlic. Cook over medium heat, stirring, 6 or 7 minutes, until the onion is lightly browned.

Stir in the broth, beans, lavender, oregano, pepper flakes, and tomato sauce. Bring to a boil over high heat. Reduce the heat and simmer, uncovered, stirring occasionally, for 10 to 15 minutes, until the carrots are tender when tested with a fork. Taste and add salt and pepper. Spoon into soup plates, garnish with chopped parsley if desired, and serve. Or, cover and refrigerate for up to 4 days, then reheat at serving time. Makes 4 main-dish servings.

Herbed Whole Roast Chicken

I grew up loving plain, old-fashioned roasted chicken, but I have to say I love this amazingly aromatic herbed version even more. It is the only way I make roast chicken nowadays, and I do hope you'll try it. If you keep a batch of the Lavender-Herb Compound Butter in the freezer, as I always do, the chicken is a breeze to make.

Tips: For quicker cooking and easier serving, or for those who prefer white meat, you can prepare bone-in, skin-on chicken breast halves the same way. Depending on their number and size, the roasting time will be 45 to 60 minutes. Use a roasting pan large enough for air to circulate around the chicken, but not so large that the pan juices run out all over the surface and evaporate.

1 (5- to 6-pound) roasting chicken

4 or 5 tablespoons Lavender-Herb Compound Butter (recipe follows)

Sea salt and freshly ground black pepper, to taste

1 small onion, quartered

Fresh lavender and thyme sprigs for garnish, optional

Preheat the oven to 425 degrees F. Rinse the chicken inside and out, then pat dry with paper towels. Remove the giblets and any excess fat. Gently loosen the skin around the breast, then work 1 tablespoon compound butter underneath the skin to baste the breast meat. Rub 2 more tablespoons butter over the entire outside of the chicken, then 1 tablespoon inside the chicken cavity. Generously sprinkle the chicken all over with salt and pepper. Put the onion in the center of a roasting pan and place the chicken on top of it.

Roast the chicken (middle rack) for 1 hour and 10 to 30 minutes, basting with the pan juices once or twice, until the juices run clear when tested by cutting deep between the thigh and breast. Let the chicken stand, covered with foil, on a deep serving platter for 15 minutes before serving and carving.

Discard the onion pieces. Skim off and discard the excess fat from the pan juices; if they look dry, stir in a tablespoon or two of water. Reheat the pan juices until hot, tasting and adding more salt and pepper and stirring in 1 tablespoon more compound butter, if desired. Garnish the chicken with fresh lavender and thyme sprigs, if desired. Spoon the pan juices over the top and serve. Makes 4 or 5 main-dish servings.

Lavender-Herb Compound Butter

I suggest always keeping fresh or dried culinary lavender around to make this delightful compound herb butter. It keeps well in the freezer, and is one the most effortless and effective ways I know to make a huge variety of savory dishes taste extraordinarily good: Add a little dollop or slice to all sorts of cooked vegetables, pan-grilled chops (especially lamb), baked fish, boiled potatoes, or broiled tomatoes. Spread it on crostini, focaccia, or slices of a crusty peasant loaf to make a distinctive and memorable gourmet garlic-herb bread. And do try it, melted, over unseasoned or lightly seasoned popcorn; it's addictive!

Tip: Don't be tempted to use olive oil in this recipe. The oils specified stay softer when chilled, keeping the compound butter more spreadable and easier to cut.

1½ tablespoons very finely minced fresh culinary lavender buds or coarsely ground dried culinary lavender buds

1½ tablespoons **each** finely minced fresh chives and fresh thyme leaves (no stems)

6 tablespoons safflower oil, sunflower oil, or canola oil

1½ teaspoons finely grated fresh lemon zest (yellow part of the peel)

½ to ¾ teaspoon finely minced fresh garlic

¾ teaspoon fine sea salt

1 cup (2 sticks) unsalted butter, just slightly soft

Combine the lavender, chives, thyme, oil, lemon zest, garlic, and salt in a food processor. Process for 1 to 2 minutes, stopping and scraping down the sides several times. Add the butter and process, scraping down the sides, just until thoroughly incorporated, about 1 minute. Turn out the compound butter onto a large sheet of plastic wrap. Pull the wrap up to fully encase the butter and twist the wrap to close it. Chill at least 1 hour so the flavors can blend and the butter can firm up.

Use immediately, or transfer the compound butter to a small nonreactive freezer-proof storage container with a tight-fitting lid. Alternatively, form the butter into sliceable log by turning it out onto a clean sheet of plastic wrap, then using the wrap to shape it into a 9-inch log and twisting the ends to secure it. Store it in a larger sturdy zip-lock bag. Use the compound butter by spooning out tablespoons or dollops, or by cutting off crosswise slices as needed. Keeps airtight and refrigerated for 1 week, or frozen for up to 3 months. Makes 1⅓ cups compound butter, or 1 9-inch log.

Ginger-Lavender Grilled (or Broiled) Salmon

Toasting is a very simple yet effective technique for bringing out and enriching the flavor of dried lavender and other herbs and spices. Here, lavender and coriander seeds are briefly toasted in a saucepan together. In warm weather it's nice to grill the salmon, but broiling is easier and can be done in any season. And the results are almost as good! Note that part of the ginger-soy mixture serves as a marinade, the other as a finishing sauce that nicely enhances the rich salmon flavor.

1½ teaspoons coarsely ground dried culinary lavender buds or very finely chopped fresh culinary lavender spikes

½ teaspoon crushed coriander seeds

2 tablespoons peanut oil, safflower oil, or other vegetable oil, plus more for the grill

1¼ teaspoons finely minced or grated peeled fresh gingerroot

⅓ cup orange juice

¼ cup **each** clover honey and reduced-sodium soy sauce

4 (5- to 7-ounce) portions boneless, skin-on salmon fillet

Lavender sprigs and lemon wedges for garnish, optional

In a 1-quart saucepan over medium heat, combine the lavender and coriander and toast, stirring constantly, until lightly toasted and fragrant, about 2 minutes. Immediately remove the pan from the heat. Stir in the oil and gingerroot, mashing the ingredients together with a spoon. Let stand for 5 minutes. Thoroughly stir in the juice, honey, and soy sauce, and let the marinade stand until cool.

Pat the salmon portions dry with paper towels. Put them in a sturdy zip-top plastic bag. Reserve ¼ cup of the marinade in a microwave-safe cup to use as a sauce; add the remainder in the plastic bag. Seal it tightly, then squeeze the bag until the salmon pieces are coated. Refrigerate for at least 30 minutes, or up to 4 hours for more intense flavor.

Brush the grill rack generously with oil. Light the coals or heat up a gas grill. (Alternatively, position the oven rack about 6 inches under the broiler, and heat the broiler to hot.) Remove the salmon from the marinade, shaking off any excess. Place the salmon pieces, skin side down, on the grill rack (or a foil-lined broiler pan). Cover the grill and cook over medium heat for 10 to 12 minutes (or broil, uncovered, for 9 to 11 minutes). Drizzle the salmon halfway through cooking with about a tablespoon of the reserved sauce, continuing to cook until the pieces just begin to flake in the center when tested with a fork. Reheat the rest of the reserved sauce until hot. Transfer the salmon to individual plates or a platter, garnishing with lemon wedges and lavender sprigs (if using). Drizzle the remaining sauce over the salmon and serve. Makes 4 main-dish servings.

Lavender-Ginger Chicken Curry

Chicken is a dinner staple at my house, and I make this very fragrant, yet uncomplicated curry often. Perhaps you weren't already aware of it, but lavender adds a nice dimension to almost any classic curry powder blend. It also has a huge affinity for ginger and allspice in both savory and sweet recipes. Here all these seasonings intermingle to enrich and mellow the curry taste.

¾ cup regular or low-sodium chicken broth, divided

2 tablespoons mild to medium-hot curry powder

2 teaspoons dried culinary lavender buds

1¼ teaspoons **each** ground allspice and finely minced peeled fresh gingerroot

1¼ to 1½ pounds trimmed boneless, skinless chicken breast halves, cut into 1-inch cubes

2 tablespoons safflower oil or sunflower oil

1 cup **each** chopped onion and coarsely chopped unpeeled sweet-tart cooking apple

1 (14-ounce) can diced tomatoes, including juice

⅔ cup dried sweetened cranberries or golden raisins (or a combination)

Sea salt and freshly ground black pepper to taste

3 to 4 cups hot cooked basmati or other long-grain white rice, for serving

Cashews, almonds, or assorted nuts for garnish, optional

Fresh lavender bloomlets for garnish, optional

In a 12-inch nonstick skillet or sauté pan, stir together about half the broth (no need to measure), the curry powder, lavender, allspice, and gingerroot. Add the chicken, stirring, until coated all over with the paste. Let stand for 5 to 10 minutes so the chicken can absorb the seasoning.

Add the oil to the skillet, stirring until the chicken is coated. Cook over medium-high heat, stirring, for 3 or 4 minutes, until the chicken lightly browns. Add the onion and apple and cook, stirring frequently, until the onion is softened, about 4 minutes.

Stir in the remaining broth, the tomatoes, and cranberries. Adjust the heat so the mixture simmers gently and cook, stirring occasionally, for 8 to 10 minutes, until it cooks down and the flavors are well blended. If the mixture starts to thicken too much, thin it with a little water. Taste and add salt and pepper as needed. Serve over rice, garnished with nuts and fresh lavender bloomlets, if desired. The dish may be made ahead, then covered and refrigerated for up to 3 days. Makes 4 main-dish servings.

Turkey Scaloppini with Lemon and Mediterranean Herbs

This healthy and zesty scaloppini features ready-to-use turkey breast cutlets instead of the veal called for in classic scaloppini. I like to serve the cutlets with pasta dressed in a light tomato and olive oil sauce and a simple green salad.

Notice that the recipe calls for Lavender-Mediterranean Herb Blend. If you don't have it on hand, make the amount needed here by stirring together 1 teaspoon **each** dried thyme leaves, dried oregano leaves, and very finely crushed or coarsely ground dried culinary lavender buds.

2 tablespoons strained fresh lemon juice, plus 1 quartered medium lemon for garnish

4 medium (4½- to 5½-ounce) turkey cutlets

1 tablespoon Mediterranean Lavender-Herb Blend (page 111)

Fine sea salt and freshly ground black pepper, to taste

6 tablespoons all-purpose unbleached flour

4 tablespoons good-quality olive oil, divided

1 medium garlic clove, peeled and halved

2 tablespoons coarsely chopped fresh parsley for garnish

Fresh culinary lavender sprigs for garnish, optional

Put the lemon juice in a 7½- by 11-inch or similar flat glass baking dish. One at a time, place the cutlets between large sheets of plastic wrap. Pound with a mallet until ¼ inch thick (or thinner) all over. Cut the pounded pieces in half, then add the cutlet pieces to the dish and turn to coat with juice on both sides. Let marinate for 10 to 15 minutes.

Drain off and discard the lemon juice. Pat the cutlets dry with paper towels. Lay out on a cutting board or mat. Sprinkle half the herb blend over all the cutlet pieces. Sprinkle with salt and pepper to taste. Sift half the flour over them. Top with plastic wrap and press down all over to embed the flour and herbs. Turn over the cutlets, then repeat the process on the second side.

In a 12- or 13-inch nonstick skillet, combine half the olive oil and one garlic half over medium heat. Cook for 1 to 2 minutes, pressing down on the garlic to infuse the oil with it. Discard the garlic. Adjust the heat to medium-high; heat the oil until hot but not smoking. Add 4 cutlet portions and cook, turning occasionally, until well browned and crispy on both sides, 4 to 5 minutes. Check the cutlets for doneness by cutting into the centers with a knife. Place them on a heat-proof dish in a low oven to keep warm. Repeat with the second batch of cutlets, using fresh garlic and oil as before. Serve all the scaloppini immediately, garnished with lemon quarters, fresh chopped parsley, and fresh lavender sprigs (if using). Makes 4 main-dish servings, 2 cutlet pieces each.

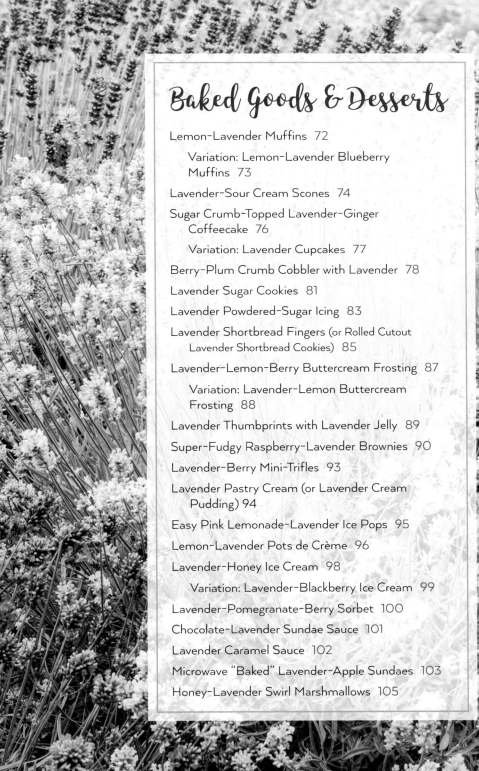

Baked Goods & Desserts

Lemon-Lavender Muffins
(or Lemon-Lavender-Blueberry Muffins)

When you start cooking with lavender you'll quickly notice its great affinity for lemon. Lemon zest always amps up lavender dishes, and lavender returns the favor in most lemon dishes, including my Lemon-Lavender Pots de Crème (page 96) and Easy Lemonade (page 23).

These muffins are large, extremely fragrant, not overly sweet, and equally at home as a breakfast treat or snack, or as an accompaniment on a brunch, luncheon, or tea table. They are delightful "plain," but if you'd like to make blueberry muffins see the variation at the end.

2 cups unbleached all-purpose white flour

Generous ¾ cup lavender sugar, homemade (page 110) or store-bought, plus 1 ½ tablespoons for topping

2 teaspoons baking powder

¼ teaspoon baking soda

Generous ½ teaspoon salt

½ cup (1 stick) unsalted butter, cut into chunks

½ cup plain nonfat or low-fat Greek-style yogurt whisked together with ⅔ cup warm water

2 large eggs, at room temperature and beaten with a fork

Generous 1 tablespoon finely grated lemon zest (yellow part of the peel)

½ teaspoon vanilla extract or ¼ teaspoon Lavender Extract (page 112)

Place a rack in the middle of the oven and preheat to 400 degrees F. Grease 12 standard-sized muffin tin cups or insert muffin cup liners.

Thoroughly stir together the flour, lavender sugar, baking powder, baking soda, and salt in a large bowl. In a microwave-safe medium bowl with a microwave oven on 50 percent power, heat the butter until soft and runny **but not boiling**, stopping and stirring every 20 seconds, until just melted. Vigorously whisk the yogurt mixture into the butter. Add the eggs, zest, and extract to the butter mixture and whisk until thoroughly blended.

Add the butter-yogurt mixture to the flour mixture, stirring with a large spoon just until the dry ingredients are evenly moistened and incorporated; don't overmix. Spoon or scoop the batter into the cups, sprinkling each with some of the 1½ tablespoons lavender sugar. (The cups should be rather full.) Evenly sprinkle any remaining sugar over the muffin tops until all is used.

Bake (middle rack) for 15 to 18 minutes or until the muffins are lightly browned on top and springy to the touch; a toothpick inserted into the thickest part of a center muffin should come out clean. Cool on a wire rack for 3 or 4 minutes. Carefully run a knife around the cups or paper liners, then remove the muffins

Tip: You'll need almost a cup of lavender sugar for these muffins. It's a good idea to keep a batch in the pantry so it's available for this recipe—and the other baked goods in this chapter.

from the pan. They are best when fresh but may be stored airtight for up to 2 or 3 days, or frozen for up to 3 weeks. Thaw, then rewarm before serving. Makes 12 standard-sized muffins.

VARIATION LEMON-LAVENDER-BLUEBERRY MUFFINS:

Spray 14 or 15 standard-size muffin tin cups with nonstick spray or line with muffin cup liners. Make the batter exactly as directed above, except as soon as the butter-yogurt mixture is lightly stirred into the flour mixture, stir together 1 cup washed and patted dry fresh blueberries with 1 tablespoon lavender sugar, then lightly fold them into the batter until evenly incorporated. Divide the batter evenly among the cups. Garnish tops with lavender sugar, then bake exactly as directed in the original recipe. Makes 14 or 15 standard-sized muffins.

Lavender-Sour Cream Scones

You'll need either my homemade or some purchased lavender sugar make these tender, buttery, not-too-sweet scones. And be sure to have extra butter for serving them, as fresh scones, like American biscuits, are at their best warm from the oven and slathered with good, sweet butter. This recipe also requires a food processor to cut the butter into the dry ingredients.

In Scotland, where scones originated and the word scone usually rhymes with **con**, many bakers add currants or other dried fruit and shape the traditional treats into rounds. But I prefer them wedge-shaped (to distinguish them from our biscuits) and enhanced with lavender. BTW, I say scone so it rhymes with **cone**. Choose whichever pronunciation you prefer!

3 tablespoons lavender sugar, homemade (page 110) or store-bought, plus 1 tablespoon for sprinkling

1¾ cups all-purpose unbleached white flour, plus ¼ cup as needed for shaping

1 teaspoon baking powder

¼ teaspoon baking soda

¼ teaspoon salt

½ cup (1 stick) cold unsalted butter, cut into small chunks

½ cup sour cream or light sour cream (don't use fat-free)

½ teaspoon Lavender Extract (page 112), optional

Preheat the oven to 400 degrees F. Line a very large baking sheet with baking parchment.

Combine the lavender sugar, flour, baking powder, soda, and salt in a food processor and process for 30 seconds. Sprinkle the butter over the dry ingredients; process in on/off pulses, checking every 20 seconds, until it is distributed and the mixture has small pea-sized butter lumps. (Evenly coating the flour mixture with the butter helps keep the scones very tender.)

Thoroughly whisk together the sour cream, 3 tablespoons room-temperature water, and the lavender extract (if using) in a medium bowl. Remove 3 tablespoons of the sour cream mixture and set aside for brushing on the scones. Gently stir the processed butter-flour mixture into the remaining sour cream mixture just until evenly blended; don't overwork the dough or the scones will be tough. With floured hands and working in the bowl, pat and smooth the dough into a flat disc; for easier handling, dust it with some of the ¼ cup additional flour.

Evenly sift about a tablespoon more flour onto a square of wax paper or baking parchment. Cut the dough disc in half, then shape each into a ball. Working with one dough portion, center it on the flour-dusted sheet. Sift a little more flour evenly over the top. Press and smooth the dough out into a 6-inch evenly

Tip: As shown in the photograph, lavender jelly is a perfect complement to scones.

thick round; if necessary, use a little more flour to aid the shaping. Brush half of the reserved sour cream mixture evenly over the dough top. Immediately sprinkle the top with half of the 1 tablespoon additional lavender sugar. Run a wide spatula under the dough to loosen it from the paper. With a greased sharp knife, cut the dough round in half, then cut each half into 3 equal wedges; lift them up and place, spaced well apart, on the baking sheet. Repeat the procedure for the second dough portion.

Bake (middle rack) for 12 to 15 minutes, until the scone tops are golden brown and a toothpick inserted in the thickest part of one comes out clean. Serve still warm with butter and a selection of jams, if desired. Makes 12 medium scones.

Sugar Crumb-Topped Lavender-Ginger Coffeecake (or Lavender Cupcakes)

Here you actually have two recipes in one! Bake the batter in a flat pan (sprinkled with a sugar-ginger crumb topping) for an exceptionally fragrant and tempting coffeecake. Or, you can prepare a totally different treat—golden, buttery Lavender Cupcakes. In this case, you'll only make the batter and bake it in muffin tin cups. Finish the cupcakes by topping with the lush berry buttercream, page 87.

BATTER

1⅔ cups unbleached all-purpose white flour

1 cup lavender sugar, homemade (page 110) or store-bought

2 teaspoons baking powder

¼ teaspoon baking soda

Generous ⅛ teaspoon salt

½ cup (1 stick) unsalted butter, cool and firm (but not hard), cut into small chunks

1 teaspoon finely grated peeled fresh gingerroot

⅓ cup plain nonfat or low-fat Greek-style yogurt, thoroughly whisked together with ½ cup water

2 large eggs plus 1 large yolk, at room temperature

2 teaspoons vanilla extract

½ teaspoon Lavender Extract (page 112), optional

SUGAR CRUMB TOPPING

6 tablespoons (¾ stick) unsalted butter, cool and firm (but not hard), cut into small chunks

⅔ cup lavender sugar, homemade (page 110) or store-bought

Place a rack in the middle third of the oven; preheat to 350 degrees F. Grease an 8½- to 9-inch square or round baking pan or coat with nonstick spray.

For the batter: Thoroughly stir together the flour, lavender sugar, baking powder, baking soda, and salt in a large mixer bowl. Add the butter and grated ginger and beat on low speed until the mixture forms very fine crumbs, about 2 minutes. In a medium bowl, using a whisk or fork, beat together the yogurt-water mixture, eggs and yolk, vanilla, and lavender extract (if using) until **very** smooth. Gradually pour the egg mixture into the flour mixture, beating on low speed until evenly incorporated. Then raise the speed to medium and beat 1 minute, occasionally scraping down the pan sides. Turn out the batter into the pan, spreading evenly to the edges. (See Variation if making cupcakes.)

For the crumb topping: In a small bowl, using a fork or a pastry blender, mash together the butter, sugar, gingerroot, and lavender extract (if using) until well blended. Cut in the flour just until fully incorporated; the mixture should still be crumbly. Sprinkle the crumb mixture evenly over the batter.

Bake for 22 to 26 minutes or until lightly browned on top and springy to the touch; a toothpick inserted into the thickest part of the center should come out clean. Cool on wire rack 15 minutes; gently run a knife around the pan edges. Cut a square pan into 9 squares, and a round pan into 8 wedges, or as desired.

1 teaspoon finely grated peeled fresh
   gingerroot

¼ teaspoon Lavender Extract (page 112),
   optional

½ cup unbleached all-purpose white flour

Tip: Both the batter and the sugar
crumb topping call for lavender sugar.
Many lavender farms and some
gourmet shops sell it, but you can
quickly make your own; the recipe is
on page 110.

The cake is best when fresh and still slightly warm, but may be
stored airtight for 24 hours, or frozen for up to 2 weeks. Let
warm to room temperature before serving. Makes 9 coffeecake
squares or 8 wedges.

VARIATION LAVENDER CUPCAKES:

Make the batter exactly as directed except omit the gingerroot
and crumb topping. Line 14 to 15 standard-size (2¼- to 2½-
inch) muffin tin cups with paper liners. Divide batter among the
cups; they will be fairly full. Bake (middle rack) at 350 degrees
F for 20 to 24 minutes, or until a toothpick tested in a center
cupcake comes out with moist crumbs; the tops will be only
lightly browned. Let cool completely. Top with Berry Buttercream
Frosting (page 87). The cupcakes are best eaten fresh, but may be
kept airtight for up to 24 hours, or frozen for up to a week. Makes
14 to 15 medium cupcakes.

Berry-Plum Crumb Cobbler with Lavender

This fruity, succulent, extremely gratifying cobbler is quite doable even if you've never worked with a cobbler dough before. That's because the crust is a buttery-crispy crumb mixture that's merely strewn over the fruit—no dough rolling or shaping is required!

The recipe calls for a combination of raspberries, blackberries, and plums—which are always tempting together, but even better with some lavender tossed in. It heightens flavor and zestiness in much the same way as lemon zest perks up some fruit dishes. If you have lavender that's in bloom, pluck off and reserve the tiny colorful flowers, or corollas, from the bloom heads, then sprinkle them over the cobbler top just before serving. They are not only eye-catching but add pleasing little pings of extra fragrance and flavor.

⅔ to ¾ cup granulated sugar (use the larger amount for very tart fruit)

2 tablespoons cornstarch

2 cups fresh red raspberries

4 cups fresh blackberries

2 cups chopped, pitted (unpeeled) sweet-tart red or black plums

2 to 4 teaspoons lemon juice, to taste

1½ teaspoons finely minced fresh culinary lavender spikes (the bloom heads), or 1½ teaspoons finely minced or coarsely ground dried culinary lavender buds

DOUGH

1⅔ cups unbleached all-purpose white flour

⅓ cup packed light brown sugar

⅓ cup granulated sugar

¾ teaspoon baking powder

¼ teaspoon salt

6 tablespoons (¾ stick) unsalted butter, melted and cooled to warm

1 teaspoon vanilla extract, **or** ½ teaspoon Lavender Extract (page 112)

1 large egg, lightly beaten and at room temperature

Ice cream or lavender whipped cream for serving, optional

Preheat the oven to 375 degrees F. Lightly coat a 9- by 13-inch baking dish (or similar-sized dish) with nonstick spray.

For the filling: Thoroughly stir together the granulated sugar and cornstarch in a large bowl. Gently stir in the berries, plums, lemon juice, and minced lavender until well blended. Spread the mixture evenly in the baking dish.

For the dough: Thoroughly stir together the flour, brown and granulated sugars, baking powder, and salt in a medium bowl. Add the melted butter, stirring until evenly incorporated. Beat the extract into the egg, then add the egg to the dough, stirring with a fork, until the mixture is blended and clumped. Sprinkle the clumps of dough evenly over the filling.

Bake (middle rack) for 30 to 40 minutes, or until well browned and bubbly on top. Transfer to a wire rack and let the cobbler cool to barely warm before serving. Garnish the top with the fresh lavender "bloomlets," if using. Top individual cobbler servings with dollops of ice cream or whipped cream, if desired. Makes 7 or 8 servings.

Tip: Ice cream is always a welcome topping for cobbler, but lavender whipped cream is also a nice touch. Just prepare the whipped cream your usual way, but substitute lavender sugar (page 110) for regular sugar.

Lavender Sugar Cookies

After visiting a number of gorgeous lavender farms in Sequim, Washington, I was inspired to capture the fragrance and flavor of culinary lavender buds in a sugar cookie and then to decorate the tops to look like lavender sprigs. (For quicker decorating, skip the icing and just sprinkle some Lavender Garnishing Sugar, page 111, over the cookies before baking them.) Any cutter shape you like will do; I think the ruffle-edged oval looks lacey and fits in with a fancy afternoon tea.

3 cups unbleached all-purpose white flour, plus a little more if needed

¾ teaspoon baking powder

½ teaspoon salt

1 cup (2 sticks) unsalted butter, slightly softened and cut into chunks

1 cup minus 2 tablespoons lavender sugar, homemade (page 110) or store-bought

1 large egg, at room temperature

1 tablespoon whole or low-fat milk

2 teaspoons vanilla extract

½ teaspoon Lavender Extract (page 112), or substitute ½ teaspoon grated fresh lemon zest

Lavender Garnishing Sugar (page 111), or store-bought crystal decorating sugar, or Lavender Powdered Sugar Icing (below).

Tip: If you've never used the rolling and cutting out method called for, it may appear a little long or complicated. But trust me, it's easier and yields much more attractive cutout cookies than any other technique I've tried. (And I've written several cookie cookbooks, so have tried many!)

In a large bowl, thoroughly stir together the flour, baking powder, and salt. Combine the butter and lavender sugar in a mixer bowl, beating on low speed until blended. On medium speed, beat until the mixture is very light and fluffy, about 2 minutes. Beat in the egg, milk, vanilla, and lavender extract (or lemon zest) until very well blended and smooth. Gradually beat or stir the flour mixture into the butter mixture to form a smooth, slightly firm, but not at all dry dough. (If the mixer motor labors, stir in the last of the flour with a spoon.) Stir in up to 3 tablespoons additional flour if the dough seems wet. Let stand 5 to 10 minutes to firm up slightly.

Divide the dough in half. Place each portion between large sheets of wax paper or parchment. Roll out each portion to a scant ¼ inch thick. Be sure the dough is evenly thick and check underside occasionally and smooth out any wrinkles. Stack the rolled portions (paper still attached) on a baking sheet. Refrigerate for about 45 minutes or until cold and firm. (Or freeze for about 25 minutes to speed up chilling.)

Preheat the oven to 375 degrees F. Generously grease several large baking sheets or coat with nonstick spray. Working with one dough portion at a time and leaving the other chilled, gently peel away, then pat the top sheet of paper back into place. (This will make it easier to lift cookies from the paper later.) Flip over the dough (still attached to the sheets) and peel off and discard the second layer. Using assorted 2½-inch to 3-inch cutters (or as desired), cut out the cookies. (If at any point the dough softens too much to handle easily, transfer the paper and cookies to a baking sheet and refrigerate until firm again.)

Using a spatula, lift the cookies from the paper and space about 1¼ inches apart on baking sheets. Re-roll any dough scraps and refrigerate until chilled. Continue cutting out cookies until all the dough is used; if the dough becomes too warm and soft for easy handling, refrigerate it briefly before continuing. If not planning to ice the cookies, sprinkle them with decorating sugar, patting down lightly.

Bake one pan at a time in the upper third of oven for 8 to 11 minutes, or until the cookies are lightly colored on top and slightly darker at edges. Rotate the pan about halfway through baking if necessary to ensure even browning. Transfer the pan to a cooling rack; let the cookies firm up a minute or two. Then, using a wide spatula, transfer them to racks and let cool thoroughly.

To spread with icing: Spread the icing onto cooled cookies using a small spreader or table knife. Work quickly and don't try to go back over the surface as the icing begins to set right away. If desired, immediately sprinkle the cookie tops with garnishing sugar, as shown in the photo at left.

To pipe with icing: Put a portion of icing in a small pastry bag fitted with a very fine writing tip, or in a paper parchment cone; don't fill the bag or cone more than half full or the icing may squeeze out the top. Pipe on decorative icing accents as desired. (It is possible to use a sturdy plastic baggie with one lower corner snipped off instead of a pastry bag and tip for drizzling or piping very simple lines, crisscrosses, or squiggles.)

Store the cookies airtight for up to 10 days or freeze, airtight, for up to 2 months. Serve at room temperature. Makes about 30 to 35 (2¾- to 3¼-inch) cookies (depending on the cutters used).

Lavender Powdered-Sugar Icing

This makes a very quick yet attractive icing for rolled sugar cookies or cutout shortbreads. If allowed to dry thoroughly (at least 12 hours), the icing sets up fairly firm, so the cookies can be stored (with wax paper between the layers) or in cool weather even shipped without sticking together. Note that the small amount of corn syrup lends the icing a nice sheen, extra smoothness, and spreadability. (If you prefer to avoid high-fructose corn syrup, choose the Karo brand.) The icing is shown on the cookies at left.

3 cups powdered sugar (sifted after measuring if lumpy), plus more if needed

3½ to 5 tablespoons Lavender Syrup (page 108), or lavender water, as needed

1 teaspoon light corn syrup

¼ teaspoon Lavender Extract (page 112), or substitute vanilla extract, or lemon extract

Food colors, preferably botanically based, as desired

Lavender Water Tip: If you don't have lavender syrup on hand, make some lavender water by pouring ⅓ cup boiling water over 1 tablespoon dried culinary lavender buds and letting the mixture steep at least 20 to 30 minutes before using. Strain the lavender water through a fine mesh sieve, pressing down on the buds to extract as much flavor as possible. The lavender water can be used immediately or readied ahead and refrigerated, if desired.

In a deep medium bowl, slowly stir or gently beat together the powdered sugar, 3 tablespoons lavender syrup (or lavender water), corn syrup, extract (if using), and food color (if using and if decorating with only one color) until well blended and smooth. Adjust the consistency by adding more lavender syrup or water to thin or more powdered sugar to thicken as necessary. For spreading, the icing should flow readily but have some body. For piping, it needs to be stiff enough to hold some shape, but thin enough to squeeze through piping tips.

To decorate with multiple colors, prepare the icing without food color, then divide it among small bowls and add drops of food color as desired. Use the icing immediately or cover and refrigerate for up to 10 days. Stir well and let it return to room temperature before using. Makes a generous 1 cup icing, enough to thinly coat or heavily accent 30 (2-inch) cookies.

To spread the icing: Spread onto cooled cookies using a small spreader or table knife. Work quickly and don't try to go back over the surface as the icing begins to set right away.

To pipe the icing: Put a portion in a small pastry bag fitted with a very fine writing tip, or in a paper parchment cone; don't fill the bag or cone more than half full or the icing may squeeze out the top. To drizzle or pipe very simple lines, crisscrosses, or squiggles, it is possible to use a sturdy plastic baggie with one lower corner snipped off.

Lavender Shortbread Fingers (or Rolled Cutout Lavender Shortbread Cookies)

Depending on how you handle this butter-laden—yet quite manageable—dough, you can create either simple yet very attractive shortbread fingers or dressy rolled, cutout shortbreads in whatever shape you fancy. It's obvious from the photo that the looks are totally different, but the taste and texture are distinctly different, too: The fingers are sturdy, toothsome, and crunchy-crisp from the crystal sugar and long, slow baking. The cutout shortbreads are slightly fragile due to their thinness, and utterly decadent due to the rich swirls of buttercream.

13 tablespoons cool but slightly soft unsalted butter, cut into chunks

½ cup plus 1 tablespoon lavender sugar, homemade (page 110) or store-bought

2 teaspoons vanilla extract

¼ teaspoon Lavender Extract (page 112), optional

Scant ½ teaspoon salt

2 cups unbleached all-purpose white flour, plus more if needed

About 3 tablespoons Lavender Crystal Garnishing Sugar (page 111) or store-bought crystal decorating sugar, for garnishing shortbread fingers; **or** Lavender-Lemon-Berry Buttercream Frosting (page 87), for decorating cutout cookies

Tip: If you don't have lavender sugar on hand, make a batch (page 110) before preparing the shortbread dough.

Position a rack in the middle of the oven; preheat to 300 degrees F.

In a large bowl with a mixer on medium speed, beat the butter, lavender sugar, vanilla, lavender extract (if using), and salt just until evenly blended, scraping down the bowl occasionally; stop beating before the butter lightens and fluffs up much. On low speed, beat in the flour just until the mixture begins to form a mass. (If the mixer motor labors, stop and stir in the flour with a large spoon.) Working in the bowl, lightly knead the dough with your hands just until it is smooth and the flour is evenly incorporated; don't overmix. If the dough is too dry to come together during kneading, work in a little water; if too soft, work in up to 3 tablespoons more flour.

To make shortbread fingers: Line a very large low-rimmed baking sheet with parchment paper. Working on a sheet of baking parchment, press or roll out the dough into an evenly thick generous 9- by 12-inch rectangle; if necessary cut and patch it to make the sides fairly even. Smooth out the dough top by topping it with parchment and lightly rolling back and forth. Then, flip over the dough (still attached to the sheets) so the smooth underside is up. Peel off the top sheet. Using a large knife, cut away and discard the uneven edges all around. Sprinkle the garnishing sugar evenly over the top and pat down lightly to embed. Cut the dough crosswise into quarters and then lengthwise into eighths to form 32 fingers. Lift up each finger with a spatula and space slightly apart on the baking sheet. (If too soft to handle easily at

Tip: If at any point the dough becomes too soft to readily cut out or transfer to baking sheets, simply slide it and the parchment onto a tray or baking sheet and refrigerate a few minutes until firm again.

any point, refrigerate the pan briefly, then continue.)

Bake (middle rack) for 20 to 25 minutes, or until the fingers are nicely browned all over. Lower the heat to 250 degrees F and bake 15 to 20 minutes longer to further crisp the fingers. Turn off the oven and let them stand in it until completely cooled.

Store the shortbread fingers airtight at room temperature for 2 weeks; or freeze them for up to 2 months and thaw at room temperature before serving. Makes 32 fingers.

To make cutout shortbread cookies: Line several large low-rimmed baking sheets with parchment paper. Divide the dough in half. Roll out one portion ¼ inch thick between sheets of parchment; be sure it is evenly thick all over. Slide the dough onto a tray or baking sheet and refrigerate until cold and firm, about 25 minutes. Repeat with the second portion.

Preheat the oven to 300 degrees F. Working with one chilled dough portion, peel off the top sheet, pat it back into place, then flip over the dough and peel off the second sheet. Cut out the cookies using desired 2- to 3-inch cutters. Lift up with a spatula and space 1½ inches apart on baking sheets.

Bake (middle rack) one pan at a time for 17 to 23 minutes, or until just lightly browned. Set the pan aside and let cookies firm up for 5 minutes, then transfer to racks using a wide spatula and let cool completely.

Using a table knife swirl on, or using a piping bag fitted with an open star tip pipe on enough buttercream frosting on each cookie to yield a ¼-inch thick layer, or as desired.

Store the frosted cookies packed flat in a single layer in an airtight container, refrigerated, for up to 3 days; or freeze them for up to 2 weeks. Serve at cool room temperature. Makes about 40 (2¼ to 2¾-inch) cutout cookies.

Lavender-Lemon-Berry Buttercream Frosting (or Lavender-Lemon Buttercream Frosting)

I love intensely-flavored, eye-catching buttercream frostings, especially ones bursting with the amazing natural taste and color of fresh lemons, bright berries, and lavender. In this recipe you get to choose among raspberries, blackberries, or blueberries; each will lend its own gorgeous pink to fuchsia hue and unique fruitiness to the basic lemon-lavender buttercream. The blackberry version is shown on the cupcakes in the photograph, the blueberry on the cookies—stunning, right!? You also have the option of omitting the berries altogether and creating a lush-tasting lavender-lemon buttercream; see the variation at the end.

Note that the technique for making this buttercream is unusual. The butter is melted together with the fruit and lavender. This, I recently discovered, is the absolute best way to infuse the frosting with the richest taste and color. The butter is then strained and chilled so it can be beaten with the powdered sugar in the normal way. The results are a remarkably deep, bright lavender-citrus-berry flavor and hue.

Tips: To ensure a smooth, succulent buttercream consistency, be sure the sieve used is fine enough that the berry seeds and lavender buds can't be forced through. Also, a little sieved pulp is usually left clinging to underside of the sieve; scrape it off and use it. And for a clean, pure frosting taste, use only fresh, top-quality unsalted butter. The recipe makes enough to frosting a batch of cupcakes, but you can double it if you want to frost a multi-layer cake.

1 cup fresh or thawed frozen blackberries, red raspberries, or blueberries combined with 1 tablespoon water

1 tablespoon dried culinary lavender buds or 2 teaspoons chopped fresh culinary lavender buds

1¼ teaspoons grated fresh lemon zest (yellow part of the peel)

½ cup (1 stick) cold unsalted butter, cut into chunks

1 tablespoon fresh lemon juice, or to taste

4 cups powdered sugar, plus more as needed

Using the bottom of a jar or a large spoon, mash the chopped berries and water, lavender buds, and lemon zest together in a 2-quart nonreactive saucepan. Place over medium-high heat and stir in the butter. Cook stirring, until the butter is completely melted and the mixture comes just to a full boil. Remove from the heat and let stand for at least 30 minutes or up to an hour to allow the flavors to mingle. Strain the butter mixture through a fine mesh sieve into a small storage container; press down to push through as much of the butter mixture as possible. Cover and refrigerate until it is chilled and firm, at least 1 hour or up to 24 hours if more convenient.

Transfer the butter mixture to a mixer bowl. Add 1 teaspoon water and the lemon juice and beat until evenly incorporated. On low speed, gradually beat in the powdered sugar. Then beat on medium speed until the buttercream has a smooth,

spreadable consistency. If it is too dry to spread, beat in a little room temperature water until spreadable; if too soft, beat in more powdered sugar. Continue beating until the buttercream is lightened and fluffy and the desired spreading or piping consistency. Note that the buttercream will stiffen slightly as it stands.

Use immediately or place in an airtight, nonreactive storage container and refrigerate for up to 4 days. Or freeze, airtight, for up to several weeks. Allow the buttercream to return to cool room temperature; beat or stir to obtain a smooth, spreadable consistency before using. Makes about 1½ cups frosting, enough for topping about 15 cupcakes or 35 small cookies.

To spread the frosting on cookies or cupcakes: Using a table knife, swirl on enough frosting on cookies or cupcake tops to yield a ¼-inch thick layer, or as desired.

To pipe the frosting: Put in a pastry bag fitted with an open star tip and pipe as desired. Serve frosted treats immediately or place in a single layer in an airtight container. Store refrigerated for up to 3 days or freeze, airtight, for up to 10 days. Let come to room temperature before serving.

VARIATION LAVENDER-LEMON BUTTERCREAM FROSTING:

Omit the berries and water from the recipe. Heat the butter-zest-lavender mixture with 2 tablespoons water and let it steep, then strain and chill the mixture exactly as directed. When beating the butter mixture with the sugar, add 2½ tablespoons water and 2 tablespoons lemon juice. Continue the remaining preparations as directed: stir in more water or powdered sugar as needed. Use the icing as is, as shown at left, or beat in a drop of yellow food dye, or a drop each of red and blue food dyes (to create a lavender shade).

Lavender Thumbprints with Lavender Jelly

These tasty thumbprint cookies look festive and always disappear quickly, but are in fact very easy and fun to make. (My grandchildren love preparing them and other thumbprints.) The lavender jelly (or lavender-infused fruit jelly) tucked into the center of each cookie makes them eye-catching, and helps keep them succulent and moist.

⅔ cup minus 1 tablespoon lavender sugar, homemade (page 110) or store-bought

1 cup (2 sticks) unsalted butter, at cool room temperature, cut into chunks

1½ teaspoons finely grated lemon zest (yellow part of the peel)

¼ teaspoon **each** baking soda and salt

1 large egg, at room temperature

2 cups plus 2 tablespoons unbleached all-purpose white flour, plus more if needed

About ⅔ cup Lavender Jelly (page 117), or substitute lavender-infused red currant, cherry, raspberry or apple jelly (see Tip)

Tip: Don't worry if you don't have lavender jelly. It's possible to quickly make a lavender-infused fruit jelly to use instead: Heat ¾ cup red currant, cherry, etc., jelly in a small saucepan just to boiling. Remove from the heat and stir in 2 to 3 teaspoons dried culinary lavender buds. Let stand while preparing the dough. Strain the jelly through a fine mesh sieve just before using it.

Position a rack in the middle third of the oven; preheat to 350 degrees F. Line 2 large baking sheets with parchment paper.

In a large mixer bowl, combine the lavender sugar, butter, lemon zest, baking soda, and salt and beat on medium speed until well blended and smooth. Beat in the egg until thoroughly incorporated.

On low speed, beat in the flour just until the mixture begins to come together. If the motor labors, stir or knead the mixture with your hands until the flour is just evenly incorporated. If it is soft and sticky, work in up to 3 tablespoons more flour. Shape the dough into a flat disc and cut into quarters. Working with one quarter at a time, and with greased hands, divide each quarter into 12 equal portions, then shape into balls. Space the balls about 2 inches apart on the baking sheets. Using a thumb or knuckle, press an indentation into the center of each cookie. Put ½ teaspoon jelly into the indentations; don't overfill them or the jelly may boil over and stick to the pans.

Bake one pan at a time (middle rack) for 12 to 16 minutes, or until the cookies are nicely tinged with brown at the edges. Transfer the pans to a wire rack and let the cookies stand until cooled to warm. Then remove them to the racks and let cool completely. Store, airtight, for up to 10 days. Or freeze airtight for 1½ months; thaw completely before serving. Makes 48 (2½-inch) thumbprint cookies.

Super-Fudgy Raspberry-Lavender Brownies

Brownies are one of America's best baking inventions. They first turned up, without any fanfare, in the 1906 edition of Fannie Farmer's *The Boston Cooking-School Cook Book*. No, Mrs. Farmer's brownies did not contain lavender. But they were rich, dark, and full of chocolate flavor, so she got us off to a very good start!

These are in Mrs. Farmer's classic brownie style (no chocolate chips, no cheesecake swirls, no icing), but with a surprising and enticing taste twist provided by raspberry jam and lavender. They are fruity and nearly as rich and deeply chocolaty as fudge—also a very good thing!

¼ cup raspberry jam or preserves, combined with 3 tablespoons water

1 cup (2 sticks) unsalted butter, cut into chunks

1 tablespoon dried culinary lavender buds

1⅔ cups unbleached all-purpose white flour

¼ cup unsweetened cocoa powder

½ teaspoon salt

2 cups granulated sugar

11 ounces bittersweet (not unsweetened) or semisweet chocolate, coarsely chopped

1 teaspoon vanilla extract

¼ teaspoon raspberry extract or Lavender Extract (page 112), optional

4 large eggs, at room temperature

Tip: The baking time depends greatly on the pan used, so check frequently for signs of doneness. In a heavy, dull metal pan that absorbs and holds heat readily, the brownies may be done in only about 20 minutes. But in a glass or shiny metal pan they may take up to 8 minutes longer. Use the toothpick test to tell.

Preheat the oven to 350 degrees F. Line a 9- by 13-inch baking pan with heavy aluminum foil; let it overhang the narrow ends. Grease or coat the foil with nonstick spray or cooking oil.

Heat the jam-water mixture and butter almost to boiling in a small saucepan, then remove from the heat. Stir in the lavender buds and let stand while readying the other ingredients. In a medium bowl, thoroughly stir together the flour, cocoa powder and salt; set aside.

Strain the butter mixture through a fine mesh sieve into a large saucepan; press down to force through as much of the mixture as possible. Stir the sugar into the saucepan. Heat on medium low, stirring constantly, just until the sugar dissolves and the mixture is hot but not boiling; don't worry if it looks curdled or oily. Remove it from the heat. Add the chocolate, stirring until completely melted. Set aside until cooled to just slightly warm (if the mixture is hot, the eggs may curdle when added).

Stir the vanilla and raspberry or lavender extract (if using) into the pan. Vigorously stir in the eggs one at a time. Stir in the flour mixture just until the batter is evenly blended. Turn out the batter into the baking pan, spreading evenly to the edges.

Bake (middle rack) for 20 minutes, then begin frequently testing for doneness: When the center top is barely firm when tapped and a toothpick inserted in the center comes out clean except for the bottom ⅛-inch (which will look wet), the brownies are done. Transfer the pan to a wire rack. Let stand until cooled to warm, about 20 minutes. For easiest cutting, refrigerate until chilled.

Using the overhanging foil as handles, carefully transfer the brownie slab to a cutting board. If desired, trim away the uneven edges using a large, sharp knife. Cutting through the foil, cut the slab in half crosswise. Carefully peel off and discard the foil from the bottoms. Cut each brownie slab into 2⅛- by 2¼-inch bars, or as desired; remember they are very rich. Wipe the knife clean with damp paper towels between cuts. Stored airtight, the brownies will keep well for 2 or 3 days. They also freeze well for up to a month. If freezing, leave the brownie slab whole, then cut into portions when partially thawed. Makes 32 (2⅛- by 2¼-inch) bars.

Lavender-Berry Mini-Trifles

A trifle is a large custard/cake/fruit/whipped-cream concoction, usually presented in a tall pedestal bowl and served as part of a dessert buffet. Here, I call for readying individual mini-trifles, which are more approachable and better suited for a sit-down meal.

Trifles originated in England. The name may refer to the fact that they were considered "trifling; frugal cooks found them a handy way to salvage stale cake or biscuits. The pastry cream, fruit, and syrup (or sherry in classic versions) do both hide and moisten the bits of cake, so this explanation seems plausible. I've used small chunks of leftover Lavender Cupcakes, or pieces of Lavender-Lemon Muffins with excellent results. If necessary, substitute any purchased or homemade sturdy vanilla cake or pound cake you wish.

Don't worry about exact proportions. Just layer a few cut-up pieces of cake, then some pastry cream, then some fruit into 5 or 6 stemmed dishes to make whatever size mini-trifles you wish. Interestingly, in the 1741 edition of her famous *The Art of Cookery Made Plain and Easy*, English cookbook author Hannah Glasse actually suggested garnishing her trifles with flowers. So, it's absolutely authentic for us modern cooks to do so!

About 2 cups coarsely crumbled or cubed leftover Lavender Cupcakes (page 77) or Lemon-Lavender Muffins (page 72), or 1-inch cubes purchased or homemade golden pound cake (crusts removed)

1 batch Lavender Pastry Cream (recipe follows)

2½ to 3 cups mixed fresh berries, such as blueberries, raspberries, and strawberries

¼ to ⅓ cup Gourmet Lavender Fruit Syrup (page 109) or Lavender Syrup (homemade, page 108 or store-bought), plus more for serving if desired

5 or 6 generous dollops of lightly sweetened whipped cream for serving

Lavender blooms or sprigs for garnish, optional

Put some cake cubes in 5 or 6 individual stemmed dessert dishes. Spoon the pastry cream, then the fresh berries over the cake to taste. If desired for convenience, cover the mini-trifles and refrigerate for up to several hours. Just before serving, drizzle them with the syrup and top with dollops of whipped cream. Garnish each dessert with a lavender bloom or sprig if you like and serve. Makes 5 or 6 servings.

Lavender Pastry Cream
(or Lavender Cream Pudding)

The same recipe is used for making a lavender pastry cream or lavender pudding. The only difference is that the pastry cream is a little thinner and reminiscent of classic custard sauce, so it requires slightly more milk. The pastry cream is called for in the Lavender-Berry Mini-Trifles on the preceding page. You can also spoon it over dishes of peaches, cherries, strawberries, or any other fruit for a light but gratifying dessert. If preparing the pudding, divide the mixture among 4 to 6 small bowls or stemmed cups. When it's well chilled, serve with dollops of whipped cream on top.

¼ cup cornstarch

¾ cup plus 2 tablespoons granulated sugar

1½ tablespoons dried culinary lavender buds

2 teaspoons finely grated lemon zest

⅛ teaspoon salt

¼ cup orange juice

7 large egg yolks, well beaten with a fork

2 cups **or** 2½ cups whole or reduced-fat milk

1 cup heavy whipping cream

2½ teaspoons vanilla extract

In a heavy, medium nonreactive saucepan whisk together the cornstarch, sugar, lavender buds, lemon zest, and salt until well blended. Whisk in the juice and egg yolks until smoothly combined. Whisk in the milk (2 cups for pudding, 2½ cups for pastry cream) and the cream. Bring the mixture to a boil over medium heat, stirring. Boil gently, stirring constantly, for a full 4 minutes, then remove from the heat. **Do not undercook**, or the pastry cream or pudding may thin out later. Stir in the vanilla.

Let the mixture stand to cool for at least 15 minutes, or up to 30 minutes for a more intense lavender flavor. (If the mixture has thickened, rewarm it just slightly, stirring, over medium-high heat.) Strain through a fine mesh sieve into a 4-cup glass measure, pressing down firmly to extract all the liquid.

If preparing pudding, divide the mixture among dessert dishes. Cover and refrigerate them at least 1 hour or until needed. If preparing pastry cream, cover the container and refrigerate for at least 1½ hours or up to 2 days before using; stir well before using. Makes about 4 cups pudding or 4½ cups pastry cream.

Easy Pink Lemonade-Lavender Ice Pops

These easy ice pops look just as tempting as store-bought but—of course—are much tastier. I like to keep them in the freezer all summer long for a really refreshing beat-the-heat family treat. If you wish to avoid artificial dyes, as I do, check the labels on the lemonade concentrate and choose a brand colored with grape or other natural fruit juices.

Tip: In case you don't have ice pop molds, the recipe includes directions for using 3-ounce plastic cups and wooden pop sticks instead. Craft stores and some discount department stores carry plain or colored wooden sticks.

¼ cup boiling water

1 tablespoon **each** dried culinary lavender buds and clover honey

1 (10- to 12-ounce) can frozen pink lemonade concentrate

1½ juice cans of water

Thoroughly stir together the ¼ cup boiling water, the lavender, and honey in a cup or small bowl. Mash the lavender against the sides using the back of a spoon several times. Let stand until cooled, about 10 minutes. Put the frozen lemonade concentrate in a large glass measure or pitcher. Strain the lavender-honey mixture through a fine mesh sieve into the concentrate; press down to extract as much liquid as possible. Thoroughly stir in the 1½ juice cans of water.

Pour the mixture into purchased ice pop molds or 6 or 7 (3-ounce) plastic cups; under-fill slightly to reduce spills and allow for the frozen mixture to expand. Add the mold inserts, or cover the cups with small squares of foil and insert sticks through tiny slits cut in the foil. Freeze the molds, or set the cups in a rimmed flat dish or tray just large enough to hold them and freeze, until frozen solid, at least 3 hours.

To unmold, dip each mold or cup in hot water for 8 to 10 seconds, then squeeze the sides to loosen the ice pop and push it out. Repeat the dipping in hot water as necessary. Don't try to remove the pops by pulling on the sticks, as they may pull right out of the pops. Serve immediately, or slip each pop into a small plastic bag, close tightly, and store in the freezer up to 2 weeks. Depending on the size of the cups or molds and how full they are, the yield will be 6 to 8 pops.

Lemon-Lavender Pots de Crème

I imagine that even if you don't speak French you have guessed that these lemony, silky-smooth custards are called "pots of cream." The name is apt, as the little desserts have an unbelievably creamy texture. The honey, lemon, lavender, and cream are supremely good together—which is why this is one of my all-time favorite desserts.

You will need 6 or 8 ovenproof ramekins, pot de crème cups, or custard cups. Ramekins that are 2½ to 3 inches in diameter and hold around ⅔ cup are ideal. The classic tempered glass custard cups are on the large side but will do, if that's what you have. You could set them on teacup saucers to dress them up a bit.

2 cups heavy (whipping) cream

¼ cup clover honey

3 to 4 tablespoons granulated sugar, to taste

2 tablespoons dried culinary lavender buds

1 tablespoon lemon zest (yellow part of the peel)

Pinch of salt

7 large egg yolks, lightly beaten with a fork

¼ cup strained fresh lemon juice

Dollops or piped swirls of sweetened whipped cream dollops for garnish, optional

Fresh lavender blooms or sprigs for garnish, optional

Fresh curls of lemon peel for garnish, optional

In a medium nonreactive saucepan, bring the cream, honey, sugar, lavender buds, lemon zest, and salt just to a boil, stirring until the honey and sugar are dissolved. Turn the heat off and let the mixture steep for at least 30 minutes, preferably 1 hour. For a more intense flavor, cover and refrigerate an hour or two longer, tasting occasionally until the desired lavender taste is achieved.

Position a rack in the middle third of the oven; preheat to 325 degrees F. Lay a tea towel in a deep roasting pan or flat baking dish large enough to hold the ramekins. Set 6 or 8 ovenproof ramekins or cups, spaced slightly apart, in the pan. Reheat the steeped lavender-cream mixture to very warm but not hot, stirring; set aside.

In a large bowl, whisk the egg yolks until very frothy and smooth. Gradually pouring in a thin stream, whisk the warm cream mixture into the egg yolks, continuing until all the cream is incorporated. Whisk in the lemon juice until evenly incorporated. Strain the custard mixture through a fine mesh sieve into a 2-cup glass measure, stirring and pressing down on the zest. Pour the mixture into the ramekins, dividing equally. Put the pan of ramekins in the oven. Immediately pour enough hot water into the roasting pan to come at least halfway up the outsides of the ramekins.

Bake for 20 minutes. Begin testing by jiggling a custard cup; as soon as the crème is set except for about the center ½ inch, the custards are done. Carefully remove the pan to a cooling rack and let stand until the custards are cool. Cover and refrigerate, covered, for up to 3 days. Let warm up just slightly before serving. Garnish with whipped cream and lavender flowers or curls of lemon peel, if desired. Makes 6 small or 8 mini-desserts.

Lavender-Honey Ice Cream
(or Lavender-Blackberry Ice Cream)

My thanks go to food show host Alton Brown for inspiring this recipe. I really wanted to create a good, easy lavender ice cream that didn't require incorporating eggs or a cooked custard base. But I wasn't having much luck. Finally, I stumbled upon his very smooth eggless vanilla ice cream recipe and used it as a starting point. The secret to the creaminess of his recipe—and mine—is in incorporating a few tablespoons of jam, which contains natural fruit pectin that prevents sugar from turning grainy when frozen. (Alton Brown used peach jam, but I use orange marmalade with the same fine results.) The exceptional flavor of this ice cream comes from combining honey, lavender, vanilla, and orange with cream; it's an ethereal match.

You can make an equally gratifying lavender-blackberry ice cream (see the variation at the end of the recipe). It will have a soft lavender-pink color, and, of course a blackberry-lavender taste.

1¾ cups whole milk

1½ cups heavy (whipping) cream

½ cup granulated sugar

⅓ cup clover honey or other mild honey, plus optional additional honey for garnishing

3 tablespoons sweet (not bitter Seville) orange marmalade

1 teaspoon vanilla extract

1 tablespoon chopped fresh culinary lavender spikes, or 1½ tablespoons dried culinary lavender buds

2 pinches fine sea salt

Chill a 1-quart storage container in the freezer. In a large non-reactive saucepan, combine the milk, cream, sugar, honey, marmalade, vanilla, lavender, and salt. Bring the mixture just to a gentle boil over medium-high heat, stirring. Gently boil, stirring, for 4 minutes. Set aside until cool, then cover and refrigerate. Let the mixture steep at least 30 minutes or up to several hours; taste occasionally, steeping until the lavender flavor suits your taste.

Strain the well-chilled mixture through a fine mesh sieve set over a bowl. Press down on the solids to force through as much cream mixture as possible; discard the solids. Put the sieved mixture in an ice cream maker and process according to the manufacturer's directions. Spoon the churned ice cream into the chilled storage container. Immediately freeze for at least 1 hour to allow the ice cream to firm up further before serving. Serve scoops drizzled with a little honey, if desired. Keeps, frozen and airtight, for up to 2 weeks. Makes 1 quart.

VARIATION LAVENDER-BLACKBERRY ICE CREAM:

Proceed as directed, except substitute 3 tablespoons blackberry jam for the marmalade. In addition, thoroughly mash 1⅓ cups fresh (or thawed frozen) blackberries with 1 teaspoon freshly grated lemon zest, then stir into the milk-cream mixture prior to cooking it.

Lavender-Pomegranate-Berry Sorbet

Lavender has a great affinity for blackberries, blueberries, pomegranate, and honey, and here they all intermingle for a complex, intensely flavorful, and brightly colored sorbet. People always like it, and I'm thrilled to tell you that *Washington Post* food editor Joe Yonan said it was probably the best fruit sorbet he'd ever tasted. Wow! (The recipe appeared in the *Post*'s food section, along with my story on cooking with lavender.) The honey not only rounds out the flavor but helps keep the sorbet texture smooth.

2 cups fresh or thawed frozen blackberries, coarsely chopped

1½ cups water

1¼ cups bottled pure pomegranate-blueberry juice, plus more as needed

½ cup clover honey, plus more to taste

6 tablespoons granulated sugar

⅓ cup fresh lime juice

1 tablespoon chopped fresh culinary lavender spikes (bloom heads) or dried culinary lavender buds

Thoroughly stir together the blackberries, water, pomegranate-blueberry juice, honey, and sugar in a medium, nonreactive saucepan. Bring to a boil, stirring. Adjust the heat so the mixture boils gently and cook until the berries are soft, 5 to 7 minutes. Stir in the lime juice and lavender and remove from the heat. Taste and thoroughly stir in a little more honey if more sweetness is desired.

Let stand at room temperature for 1 hour (fresh lavender will infuse much more quickly than dried buds). Taste and when the lavender flavor suits you, strain the mixture through a fine mesh sieve into a 4-cup measure. Press down with a spoon to extract as much liquid as possible. (For most intense lavender flavor, refrigerate, tasting occasionally, for up to 3 hours before straining.) If necessary, stir enough additional pomegranate-blueberry juice into the measure to yield a generous 3¾ cups. Refrigerate, covered, until very well chilled. Chill a storage container to hold the finished sorbet.

Process the mixture in an ice cream maker following the manufacturer's directions. Immediately put the sorbet in the chilled freezer container and freeze until firm again, at least 1 hour, before serving. Store in the freezer for up to 2 weeks. Makes a generous 1 quart.

Chocolate-Lavender Sundae Sauce

Occasionally I just *have to have* a little chocolate-and-lavender treat. That's why a batch of this rich, creamy, full-flavored sundae sauce is usually stashed in my refrigerator. When the craving hits, I grab a scoop or two of ice cream (also kept on hand), drizzle over this sauce, and dig in. I recommend that you do the same!

Tip: The percentage of cacao (the dark, starchy, bitter part of chocolate) of the chocolate is important because it affects how thick and how sweet the sauce will be. A chocolate labeled 72 percent cacao will be about 27 percent sugar, while one labeled 50 percent cacao will be about 48 percent sugar. So, just by choosing the chocolate carefully, you can take the sauce in the direction of robust and dark or mild and semisweet to suit your taste.

1¼ cups boiling water

1½ tablespoons dried culinary lavender buds

6 ounces bittersweet (60 to 72 percent cacao) or semisweet (50 to 60 percent cacao) chocolate, chopped

¼ cup unsweetened cocoa powder, sifted after measuring if lumpy

½ cup granulated sugar

6 tablespoons unsalted butter, slightly softened and cut into chunks

1 teaspoon vanilla extract

¼ teaspoon Lavender Extract (page 112), optional

Stir together the boiling water and lavender. Let steep for at least 10 minutes, or up to 20 minutes for a pronounced lavender flavor. Strain the lavender water through a very fine sieve into a microwave-safe 2-cup glass measure, pressing down to extract all the liquid. If necessary, add enough water to yield 1¼ cups.

Combine the chopped chocolate, cocoa powder, and sugar in a food processor. Process until the chocolate is finely chopped. Microwave the lavender-water on 50 percent power, stopping and checking every 20 seconds, until steaming hot but not boiling. With the processor motor running, slowly add the hot lavender liquid through the feed tube, processing until the mixture is very smooth and well-blended. Continuing to process, add the butter, then the vanilla and lavender extract (if using). Process until the mixture is smooth. If it is very thick, thin it with a bit more hot water as it will thicken further as it stands. Use immediately or cover and refrigerate for up to 10 days. Microwave on low power, stirring frequently, to bring the sauce back to room temperature. Thin it with a little more hot water if necessary before serving. Makes about 2 cups sauce.

Lavender Caramel Sauce

Try this to-die-for lavender caramel sauce over Lavender-Honey Ice Cream (page 98), with Microwave "Baked" Lavender-Apple Sundaes (recipe follows), or over poached pears or peaches. Warmed up slightly, it also makes a wonderful dipping sauce for fresh apple slices. And, I've been known to sneak a little spoonful of it from the refrigerator and eat it straight for dessert.

Tip: If you prefer to avoid high fructose corn syrup, use the Karo brand. But don't omit the corn syrup as it keeps the sauce from turning grainy and sugary.

1½ cups heavy (whipping) cream, divided

1½ to 2 tablespoons dried culinary lavender buds

1 teaspoon vanilla extract

1¼ cups packed light or dark brown sugar

1 cup light corn syrup

5 tablespoons butter, preferably unsalted, cut into chunks

Pinch of sea salt

Bring ½ cup of the heavy cream to a boil in a small saucepan over high heat. Stir in the lavender buds and vanilla and set aside to steep.

Thoroughly stir together the remaining 1 cup cream, the sugar, corn syrup, butter, and salt in a heavy 4-quart nonreactive pot or saucepan. Bring to a boil over medium-high heat, stirring constantly with a long-handled wooden spoon. When the mixture is boiling briskly, wipe any sugar from the pan sides using a pastry brush dipped in warm water (or a damp paper towel). Thoroughly wash all sugar from the stirring spoon.

Adjust the heat so the mixture boils briskly and cook, occasionally stirring and scraping the pan bottom. As the mixture starts to thicken and turns a rich medium caramel color (like caramel candies) stir more frequently; reaching this stage will take at least 7 or 8 minutes. Remove from the heat. Strain the lavender-infused cream through a fine mesh sieve into the caramel mixture. Bring it back to a full boil for 1 minute. Then let the sauce cool to warm.

Use the sauce immediately or refrigerate, tightly covered, for up to 10 days. Rewarm on low power in a microwave oven; stir and check the consistency every 30 seconds as the caramel should not boil again. If the sauce is very thick, thin it slightly by stirring in a little warm water. Makes about 2 cups sauce.

Microwave "Baked" Lavender-Apple Sundaes

It's hard to believe that such a simple recipe could deliver such delectable results. Fast, fuss-free microwave "baking" not only reduces the usual oven baking time from about 45 minutes to 12, but yields moister, plumper apples with enough sweet, bubbly lavender-scented juice to use as a sundae sauce. For "plain" sundaes, simply top the apples and ice cream with the apple juices. For fabulously decadent ones, spoon over my warm Lavender Caramel Sauce (previous page) as well. Heavenly!

Keep in mind that different varieties and sizes of apples will cook at different rates and some **are much better for baking** whole than others. Several of my favorites are suggested below; I skip Granny Smiths because they come out too sour and drab-looking, and Macintoshes because they slump and turn applesauce-y.

Tip: If you don't have homemade or purchased lavender sugar on hand, make what you need here by combining 1 teaspoon dried culinary lavender buds and ¼ cup granulated sugar in a food processor. Process for 3 or 4 minutes until the lavender is ground fairly fine. Strain the sugar through a fine sieve mesh sieve, discarding the strained out bits.

4 large (9- to 11-ounce) washed, full-flavored tangy-sweet apples, such as Honey Crisp, Rome, Stayman Winesap, Golden Delicious, or Braeburn

4 tablespoons lavender sugar, homemade (page 110) or store-bought; or see tip

4 tablespoons apple juice or water

Scoops of Lavender-Honey Ice Cream (page 98) or store-bought vanilla ice cream, for serving

Lavender Caramel Sauce (page 102), optional, for serving

Using an apple corer (or paring knife if necessary), remove the apple cores, leaving an open channel running from the top through the base of the apples. Arrange the apples upright in deep-sided individual baking dishes or in an 8-inch square (or similar) deep microwave-safe glass dish. Don't crowd or their juices may bubble over the sides. Spoon a tablespoon of sugar over each apple. Drizzle 1 tablespoon apple juice (or water) over each apple. Put the dishes or dish in the microwave oven; top with a microwave cover or lid.

Microwave the apples at 100 percent power. Baking time can vary considerably: Start checking for doneness by piercing the apples in the thickest part at 7 minutes, then every 2 minutes until tender, up to 12 or 13 minutes total for very large apples. Let the apples stand a few minutes before serving. If they were not in individual dishes, transfer to individual bowls. Top the servings with scoops of ice cream, then spoon over the apple juices and Lavender Caramel Sauce, if using. For convenience the apples may be baked ahead and refrigerated for up to 3 days; rewarm at 50 percent power in the microwave. Makes 4 servings.

Honey-Lavender Swirl Marshmallows

When I first prepared homemade marshmallows I was astonished at how incredibly succulent and flavorful they were. Even now, I'm always amazed at how much lighter, more tender, and tastier they are than store-bought. And *these* marshmallows are particularly delectable due to the addition of honey and lavender, a pairing either devised for or by the gods!

1 cup water, divided

2 tablespoons dried culinary lavender buds

2 teaspoons grated lemon zest (yellow part of the peel)

2 tablespoons plus 1 teaspoon (3 to 4 packages) unflavored gelatin

About ⅓ cup powdered sugar for dusting dish and marshmallows

1¼ cups granulated sugar

⅔ cup light corn syrup

⅓ cup clover honey or other mild-flavored honey

1 pinch of salt

Natural botanical blue food color packets, as needed, dissolved with 1 teaspoon water and a tiny drop of lemon juice; or drops of purple petrochemical food dye

Heat ⅓ cup of the water until almost boiling in a small non-reactive saucepan. Remove from the heat, then stir in the lavender and lemon zest. Let stand at least 15 minutes, or up to 30 minutes for the fullest lavender flavor.

Meanwhile ready the other ingredients. In a small bowl, sprinkle the gelatin over the remaining ⅔ cup cold water. Let stand, stirring occasionally, until the gelatin softens and absorbs the water, at least 6 or 7 minutes. Spray a 9- by 13-inch flat baking dish with nonstick spray. Line with parchment paper, allowing the paper to slightly overhang the narrow ends. Very evenly coat the paper with nonstick spray. Evenly sift a light layer of powdered sugar onto the paper; the marshmallow will stick to any spots missed.

Place a very fine sieve over a measuring cup. Strain the steeped lavender mixture, pressing down hard to force through all the liquid. If you have less than ¼ cup, add enough water to yield ¼ cup.

In a 4-quart (or similar) heavy saucepan over medium-high heat, stir together the lavender liquid, granulated sugar, corn syrup, honey, and salt until well blended. When the sugar dissolves, raise the temperature and bring the mixture to a full, rolling boil, stirring. Continue boiling, uncovered, for 20 seconds. Stir in the gelatin mixture and boil, stirring, for 30 seconds longer. Remove from the heat and continue stirring until the gelatin completely dissolves.

Pour the mixture into a large mixer bowl. Using a whisk attachment if available and gradually raising the mixer speed

Tip: For dishes that need brightening with food color I skip the usual petrochemical food dyes and use only additive-free botanical colorants. Should you wish to follow suit, the Color Garden botanical spirulina blue coloring packets (available on the Internet) deliver a brighter, clearer blue shade than most other brands. It's easy to turn spirulina blue to lavender or purple just by mixing in a tiny drop of lemon juice. Don't overdo the lemon juice though, or the blue can change to pink!

from low to high, beat until the mixture is lightened, fluffy, and beginning to stiffen, about 5 minutes. Immediately remove 1 cup of marshmallow and mix together in a bowl with drops of food color until well blended and a medium purple shade. Continue beating the large bowl of marshmallow until it is stiff instead of runny, about 2 minutes. Using a nonstick spray-coated rubber scraper, lightly swirl some of the purple mixture into the plain mixture; don't overmix. Then lift up more marshmallow from underneath, and add in more purple swirls. Continue lifting the marshmallow and folding in more swirls until all the colored mixture is used and the marshmallow is rippled here and there throughout.

Immediately turn out the swirled marshmallow mixture into the prepared baking dish, quickly spreading evenly to the edges. Evenly sift a thin layer of powdered sugar over the surface. Carefully coat a second sheet of parchment paper with nonstick spray; press the sprayed sheet down on the marshmallow surface. Refrigerate at least 6 hours, or up to 24 hours; the marshmallow slab will be easier to handle if left the full 24 hours. If it still seems sticky, freeze for about 30 minutes to facilitate cutting.

To cut the marshmallows: Evenly sift powdered sugar onto a large clean cutting board. Peel off the top sheet of parchment from the chilled marshmallow slab, then lay the slab, peeled side down, on the sugared surface. Peel off the second sheet of parchment paper and sift more powdered sugar over the top. Using lightly greased kitchen shears or a lightly greased large, sharp knife, trim off and discard uneven edges all around. Cut the slab crosswise into 10 portions and lengthwise into 8 to form 80 marshmallows (or cut as desired for larger or smaller marshmallows). Dust all the cut surfaces of the marshmallows with powdered sugar to reduce their stickiness. As necessary, clean off the knife and re-grease. Place the marshmallows in a powdered sugar-dusted airtight flat container with wax paper between the layers. Store, refrigerated, for up to 2 weeks; or freeze for up to 2 months. Makes 80 marshmallows, about 1¼- by 1-inch each.

Pantry & Refrigerator Staples

Lavender Syrup

Lavender recipes are not as common in antique cookbooks as you might suppose. In really old volumes, lavender is sometimes call *spike*, or *spikenard*, so it's easy to miss. And often lavender recipes are tucked among the medicinal or herbal remedies. One such "receipt" is in the 1832 *The Cook's Own Book*, by Mary Middleton Rutledge Fogg. To make "Lavender Drops" she called for filling a quart bottle with "blossoms of lavender," and pouring over "as much brandy as it will contain...." She recommended a few drops combined with a bit of sugar for "nervous cases." I suspect the brandy had more to do with any calming effect than the lavender!

This syrup may or may not calm your nerves, but it has a delightful herbal-floral taste and is extremely versatile. Drizzle it over almost any fruit, ice cream, or sorbet to add a touch of haunting flavor and sweetness. Or add a little to vinaigrettes, marinades, and pan sauces to help smooth and mellow the flavors.

Tips: If your lavender buds are a bright blue or purple, the syrup will have a purple or amber tinge; if they are pale, the syrup will be colorless or have just a faint tinge. To brighten up its color, just add a drop of lemon juice; the acidity will cause the lavender color pigments to show up more and turn fuchsia or bright pink. The syrup will keep best if you carefully sterilize the sieve, spoon, and storage bottle or jar and lid. Always store the syrup in the refrigerator.

2 cups granulated sugar

2 cups water

2 to 2½ tablespoons dried culinary lavender buds, to taste

Stir together the sugar and water in a medium nonreactive saucepan over medium heat. Bring to a boil, stirring, then adjust the heat so the mixture boils gently. Cook, stirring occasionally, for 4 minutes to thoroughly dissolve the sugar. Stir in the lavender buds. Remove from the heat and let stand, covered, so the lavender can fully infuse the syrup, at least 1 hour or up to 6 hours, tasting occasionally until the desired lavender flavor has been reached.

Strain the syrup through a very clean fine mesh sieve into a clean saucepan. Bring to a boil and boil 1 minute. Pour into a sterilized bottle or jar. Press down firmly to force through all the liquid. Let cool, then refrigerate. The recipe can be doubled if desired. Store the syrup, airtight, in the refrigerator for up to 3 months. Makes a generous 2 cups syrup.

Gourmet Lavender-Fruit Syrups

This recipe includes one preparation method, but two slightly different ingredient lists. Use the first ingredient list to team lavender with stone fruits or berries, the second list when combining lavender with citrus fruit. In either case the resulting lavender-fruit syrup will be spectacular: The lavender works to round out and heighten the distinctive flavor of each fruit, and each fruit contributes its own jewel-like color and aroma to the lavender. A raspberry syrup is are shown on page 28.

You'll find dozens of uses for these beautiful syrups: Drizzle over mixed fruit compotes, berries, or plates of sliced nectarines or melons. (Add a sliver of prosciutto and or creamy cheese to the melon plate for a splendid appetizer!) Team up with scoops of ice cream along with the fruit featured in the syrup for simple but spectacular sundaes (as shown in the photograph on the title page). Spoon a little into the skillet after cooking chicken, duck, pork, or lamb to create a quick, savory pan sauce or glaze. Add a splash to soft or hard beverages, especially those featuring lemon, lime, orange, peach, or ginger flavors.

BERRY OR STONE FRUIT SYRUP

2 cups granulated sugar

2 cups water

½ cup finely chopped fresh blackberries, raspberries, strawberries, blueberries, cranberries, or cherries; or chopped pitted (unpeeled) peaches, nectarines, plums, or apricots

2 tablespoons dried culinary lavender buds

1 tablespoon fresh lemon juice

CITRUS SYRUP

2 cups granulated sugar

2 cups water

½ cup chopped fresh pulp and juice from oranges, blood oranges, Minneola tangelos, bitter (Seville) oranges, tangerines, lemons, limes, or grapefruits

2 tablespoons dried culinary lavender buds

1 teaspoon freshly grated zest (colored part of the peel) of the citrus used

Stir together the sugar, water, and fruit in a medium nonreactive saucepan over medium heat. Bring to a boil, stirring, then adjust the heat so the mixture boils gently. Cook, stirring occasionally, for 5 to 10 minutes, until the fruit is soft. Stir in the lavender buds, lemon juice (if using), and citrus zest (if using). Set aside, covered, and let the syrup infuse for at least 1 hour or up to 4 hours, tasting occasionally until the desired flavor is reached.

Strain the syrup through a fine mesh sieve into a large measure; press down on the solids to push through as much liquid as possible. If you have less than 2 cups syrup, add enough water to make 2 cups. Rinse out the saucepan. Add the sieved syrup, bring back to a boil, and boil for 1 minute. Cool slightly. Pour into a clean (preferably sterilized) storage bottle, cover airtight, and refrigerate for up to 3 months. Makes a generous 2 cups syrup.

Lavender Sugar (or Lavender Vanilla Sugar or Lavender Powdered Sugar)

I try to always keep lavender sugar (or the vanilla variation) in my pantry. It's just so handy! Here are just a few easy, tasty uses: Sprinkle on sliced fruit, berries, or grapefruit halves. Use to sweeten citrus-flavored orange pekoe or peppermint tea. Substitute for regular sugar to deepen flavor in pound cakes, brownies, muffins, and such. Mix with a little cinnamon for an exceptional cinnamon toast topping. (And note that it is called for in many of the baked goods in this book.)

2 cups granulated sugar, divided
2 tablespoons dried culinary lavender buds

Tips: It's easy to double this recipe, but remember that once lavender buds are pulverized their heady volatile oils are released and begin to fade away. So make only what you think you'll use up within a few months. If you don't care for noticeable flecks in your lavender sugar, make it with pale-colored buds. The pale pink and gray-blue culinary lavenders are just as flavorful as the bright purple kinds, but will blend in better.

In a food processor or spice grinder, grind ½ cup sugar and the lavender until very fine; this will take 4 to 5 minutes in a processor, about 20 seconds in a spice grinder. Push the ground sugar mixture though a very fine mesh sieve, discarding the sieved lavender bits (or saving them for another use). Thoroughly stir the sieved lavender sugar into the remaining 1½ cups sugar until evenly incorporated. (Or, grind the two together in a processor until blended.) Store airtight in a jar in a cool spot for up to 4 or 5 months. Makes 2 cups lavender sugar.

VARIATION: LAVENDER VANILLA SUGAR
Chop a 1-inch-long piece of *dry* vanilla bean into small bits and add to the processor or grinder along with the lavender. (Don't use a soft or moist piece of vanilla bean, as it will make the sugar wet and prone to clumping.) Once the mixture is ground, sieve out both the lavender and vanilla bean bits.

VARIATION: LAVENDER POWDERED SUGAR
Substitute powdered sugar for the granulated sugar. Use lavender powdered sugar to dust the tops of desserts, or to add a coating to cookies, confections, and such. Do not try to substitute lavender powdered sugar for an equal amount of lavender granulated sugar as the powdered is only about half as dense and therefore much less sweet.

Lavender Crystal Garnishing Sugar

Lavender garnishing sugar (shown on page 84) adds a touch of sparkly lavender color and flavor, plus a little crunch to cookies, muffins, coffeecakes, and other baked goods. Look for clear crystal decorating sugar in gourmet shops, some craft shops, and discount department stores (in the cake decorating section).

Tip: Some culinary lavender buds are a bright or dark purple, others a pale pink or blue shade. The pale buds are a better choice if you want to avoid dark lavender flecks in your garnish.

½ cup coarse clear or white crystal sprinkling sugar or sparkling sugar

1 teaspoon ground or finely crushed dried culinary lavender buds

¼ teaspoon Lavender Extract (page 112) or water

1 drop purple food color, preferably botanically based (or 1 tiny drop each red and blue food color)

Turn the oven on for 2 minutes, then immediately turn it off again; it should be barely warm. Line a baking sheet with aluminum foil. Put the crystal sugar in a small, deep bowl. Sift the lavender through a fine mesh sieve into the sugar. Combine the lavender extract or water and the food color. Stir into the sugar mixture until thoroughly blended. Spread the sugar out on the baking sheet. Let stand in the oven, stirring several times, for at least 1 hour or up to several hours, until completely dry. Store airtight in a cool, dark spot for up to a year. Makes ½ cup garnishing sugar.

Mediterranean Lavender-Herb Seasoning Blend

This simple, versatile seasoning is what I use instead of the familiar commercial Italian Seasoning mix; the homemade blend is much more flavorful than store-bought. Note that this blend is not a substitute for herbes de Provence; its flavor is quite different. I call for grinding the ingredients in a food processor because most home cooks have one. (If you have a spice grinder, pulse, checking every few seconds, until ground fairly fine.)

2 tablespoons dried culinary lavender buds

2 tablespoons dried thyme leaves

2 tablespoons dried oregano leaves

Combine the lavender, thyme, and oregano in a food processor. Process for 3 to 4 minutes or until the lavender is ground fairly fine. Store the mixture airtight in a cool spot in a glass jar or spice bottle. For fullest flavor use it within 9 months. Makes about ⅓ cup herb blend.

Lavender Extract (or Lavender-Vanilla Extract)

I urge you to make your own lavender extract. It's a snap, and it will be much tastier than store-bought. That's because fresh or dried lavender blooms are used as is, which preserves all their glorious complex flavor elements. Most commercial extracts are flavored with lavender essential oil, and the heat from the distilling process diminishes and alters some of the herb's most pleasing flavor compounds.

If you have a piece of vanilla bean pod handy, consider creating a lavender-vanilla extract instead. The vanilla bean doesn't even have to be fresh, moist, or newly purchased. I've salvaged ones already split and scraped out and ones too hard and brittle to use in baking!

Enough fresh or dried culinary lavender bloom heads or sprigs to fill a 2- to 4-ounce (or similar) glass bottle

Enough good-quality vodka or grain alcohol to fill the bottle

1 (3- to 3½-inch-long) piece of whole vanilla bean, optional

Rinse, then pat the lavender dry. Trim off the stems as needed and stuff the bottle full with the lavender blooms or sprigs; use a fondue fork if the neck is narrow. Fill the jar to within ½ inch of the top with the vodka or grain alcohol; make sure all the lavender is submerged. Insert a piece of vanilla bean (if using). Cover tightly and let the extract stand at least 1 week before using.

If desired, leave the lavender (and vanilla, if using) in the bottle to steep, replenishing the alcohol as needed. (Alternatively, strain the extract through a fine mesh sieve, discard the lavender (and vanilla), and return the extract to the bottle. Then, if desired, add a new lavender sprig or two for a gourmet look.) Store the extract airtight in a cool spot. For fullest flavor use within 1 year. Makes 2 to 4 ounces extract, depending on the bottle used.

Tips: You'll need a 2- to 4-ounce glass bottle that has a tight-fitting glass, cork, or plastic top; the alcohol can corrode a metal lid and will evaporate rapidly if the top is loose.

Lavender Aged Balsamic Vinegar

I once bought a fancy (pricey!) bottle of aged lavender-balsamic vinegar at a gourmet shop not knowing what to expect. It was delectable! And there's a reason: the herb's complex fruity and floral notes intermingle beautifully with the deep, concentrated natural sweet and sour elements of the cooked juice of late-harvested Lambrusco or Trebbiano grapes. Drizzle a few drops of the vinegar over the same dishes you would dress with the "plain" version—figs, berries, plums, creamy cheeses, panna cottas and similar desserts.

8 to 10 spikes (bloom heads) fresh or dried culinary lavender

About ⅓ cup aged balsamic vinegar, or as needed

Tip: A 3-ounce (or similar) bottle or jar works well, but use whatever is on hand; just be sure it has a nonreactive stopper or lid.

Trim off the lavender stems so the sprigs fit the bottle or jar used. Tuck them into the bottle, then fill it with the vinegar until they are covered. Push them down into the vinegar if necessary. Let stand at least 10 days before using. Leave the lavender spikes in the bottle and occasionally top it off with more vinegar or, if preferred, remove and discard the lavender after 2 or 3 weeks. Keeps, airtight in a cool spot, for up to 1 year. Makes about ⅓ cup lavender-aged balsamic vinegar.

Lavender-Herb Tea Blend

I call this simple brew of lavender buds and either chamomile or peppermint leaves a tea, but purists will tell you that it's in fact a tisane—that is, a beverage served like tea, but not actually made from tea leaves.

Use **loose** dried peppermint leaves or dried chamomile flowers, not products in tea bags. (These latter are often ground too fine to use in a tea ball or infuser basket.)

¼ dried culinary lavender buds

¼ cup loose dried peppermint leaves or dried coarsely chopped chamomile flowers

Stir together the lavender and peppermint or chamomile leaves. Keeps, stored airtight in a cool, dry spot for up to 1 year. Makes ½ cup lavender-herb tea blend.

For each large cup of tea: Put 1½ teaspoons of the tea blend in a tea ball or small infuser basket in a mug or large tea cup. Pour 1 cup just barely boiling water into the mug. Let steep at least 2 minutes or longer for a stronger tea. Sweeten with honey, lavender sugar, or gourmet lavender-citrus syrup, page 109, if desired. Serve with lemon wedges if you wish.

Lavender Hot Cocoa Mix

Like vanilla, lavender subtly enhances many chocolate and cocoa recipes. Here, it doesn't stand out, but it enriches and deepens the chocolaty flavor, so the cocoa tastes even better than usual! I love to keep a jar of lavender cocoa mix around to fix myself and my family a quick, satisfying cup. Actually, I often double or triple the recipe; jars of the mix make thoughtful gifts for all sorts of occasions. (If you do give out the mix for presents, remember to attach directions for making the cocoa!)

1 cup granulated sugar, divided

3 tablespoons dried culinary lavender buds

¾ cup unsweetened cocoa powder (**not** ready-to-use cocoa drink mix)

Tip: Be sure to use unsweetened cocoa powder, not a chocolate drink mix. Labels should say "pure baking cocoa," or "100 percent cacao," or "unsweetened cocoa powder."

Combine ½ cup of the sugar and the lavender buds in a processor. Process for 4 or 5 minutes, until the lavender is very finely ground. Push the mixture through an extra-fine mesh sieve, discarding the sieved lavender bits. Return the sieved sugar-lavender mixture to the processor. Add the remaining ½ cup sugar and the cocoa powder. Process for 1 to 2 minutes, stopping and stirring once or twice, until the ingredients are thoroughly blended. Put the cocoa mix in an airtight storage jar (or jars). Keeps for up to 1 year. Makes 1¾ cups cocoa mix.

To make a serving of cocoa: Put ¼ cup hot tap water in a 10- to 12-ounce microwave-safe mug. Stir in 2 tablespoons cocoa mix until well blended. Stir in 1 to 1¼ cups milk; use the larger amount for a milder cocoa. Heat the mug in the microwave on 100 percent power, stopping and stirring every 20 to 30 seconds, until the cocoa is piping hot; do not boil. Float Lavender Marshmallows (page 105) on top, if desired. Stir again, then serve immediately. Makes 1 large (1¼- to 1½-cup) serving.

Herbes de Provence

No wonder we associate herbes de Provence with the lavender growing regions of France. Decorative jars and packets of it are sold everywhere and are a favorite tourist souvenir. But lavender is actually a fairly recent addition to the classic herbes de Provence seasoning blend. The landmark 1910 cookbook *La Cuisinière Provençale* did include herbes de Provence, but it lacked lavender. Then, in the mid-20th century, purveyors began to add it, perhaps to entice those visiting the lavender fields. This turned out to be both a good marketing and culinary idea.

My own heady blend is incredibly fragrant and excellent with all sorts of dishes. Combine it with a little oil and rub it into chicken, turkey, pork, lamb, and fish. Or mix it with melted butter or a little glug of olive oil to season roasting potatoes, beans, mushrooms, or broiled tomatoes.

Tip: If you don't have a mortar and pestle, crush the fennel seeds by sealing them in a small, heavy-duty plastic bag and pounding with the back of a heavy spoon or kitchen mallet until thoroughly pulverized.

1½ tablespoons **each** dried culinary lavender buds and dried rosemary leaves

1 tablespoon fennel seeds, crushed until fine using a mortar and pestle

1 tablespoon plus 1 teaspoon **each** dried marjoram leaves and dried thyme leaves

1 tablespoon **each** dried oregano leaves and dried tarragon leaves

Grind the lavender, rosemary, and fennel seed in a food processor for 5 minutes, or until fairly finely ground. Add the marjoram, thyme, oregano, and tarragon and process until well combined, about 2 minutes longer. Store in an airtight bottle or jar. Best used within 1 year. Makes about ½ cup herbes de Provence.

Latin-Inspired Lavender-Spice Blend

Versatile and extremely savory and fragrant, this seasoning blend is excellent for grilling or roasting chicken pieces, pork or lamb chops, or a whole pork loin or lamb roast. For every (boneless) pound of meat, rub 1 to 1½ tablespoon of the mixture over the meat surface. Smaller pieces such as chops need only to stand for 5 to 10 minutes, but for best flavor, cover larger cuts with plastic wrap and refrigerate for at least half an hour before pan grilling, grilling, or roasting.

3 tablespoons ground coriander

1 tablespoon ground cumin

1 tablespoon very finely crushed or coarsely ground dried culinary lavender buds

1 teaspoon granulated sugar

½ teaspoon **each** smoked sea salt (or regular sea salt, if necessary) and ground black pepper

¼ teaspoon dried garlic granules or garlic powder

Thoroughly stir together the coriander, cumin, lavender, sugar, sea salt, pepper, and garlic in a small deep bowl until evenly blended. Store in an airtight jar in a cool, dark spot. Keeps for up to 1 year. Makes about ⅓ cup seasoning blend.

Gourmet Peppercorn-Lavender Pepper Mill Blend

It's so simple, it hardly counts as a recipe, but this pepper blend shows off the great affinity of lavender buds and gourmet peppercorns and, more important, provides a handy way to use them together to enhance dishes. I keep a pepper mill of the blend right by the stove at all times, and routinely add extra fragrance, color, and zip by incorporating a few grinds into all the dishes that I used to season with "regular" pepper. The mixture is especially good with sweet potatoes and tomato soup.

Be sure to use a "rainbow" pepper blend containing green, white, black, and pink peppercorns.

¼ cup store-bought 4-peppercorn blend

1 tablespoon dried culinary lavender buds, preferably purple or blue buds

Stir together the peppercorns and lavender. Put in a peppermill. Grind over salads, meats, vegetables, or any other dishes where fresh ground pepper might be used. Keeps airtight in a cool, dark spot for up to 1 year. Makes ⅓ cup peppercorn–lavender blend.

Lavender Jelly

England's Queen Elizabeth I is said to have asked for lavender conserve on her dining table every day. Nobody has ever found her chef's recipe, but "conserves," ranging from simple lavender flower-sugar blends to cooked lavender preserves similar to modern jams, were around in her era. One such recipe, called "Conserve of Flowers of Lavender," appears in *The Queen's Delight: The Art of Preserving, Conserving and Candying*, printed in London in 1671.

Like Her Majesty, I always want a lavender spread, such as this jelly, on my table. Brightened up with lemon but not overshadowed by it, the jelly has an elusive, irresistible fruit-spice flavor. My husband and I *must have it* on our morning toast or scones. Depending on the brightness of the lavender buds, the jelly can range in color from pinkish-blush to amber (see a photo on page 75), but the taste will be lovely either way.

If you're new to jelly making, keep in mind that precisely the right amounts of sugar, acid (from the lemon juice), and liquid are necessary for the natural jelling agent, fruit pectin, to set up well, so measure and follow the cooking procedure carefully. On the rare chance your jelly nevertheless comes out on the saucy side, enjoy it spooned over yogurt or ice cream, or French toast or pancakes.

2¾ cups water

2 to 3 tablespoons dried culinary lavender buds

1 teaspoon finely grated fresh lemon zest (yellow part of the peel)

⅓ cup plus 1 tablespoon fresh lemon juice, strained

3½ tablespoons traditional or classic powdered pectin (do not use low-sugar pectin)

3¼ cups granulated sugar

Tips: Check the use-by date to be sure the pectin is fresh. Use the very large pot specified or the jelly may boil up over the sides..

Bring ½ cup water just to boiling in a nonreactive saucepan. Remove from the heat and stir in the lavender and lemon zest. Let stand to steep at least 1 hour, or up to 12 hours (refrigerated), for a more intense flavor. Strain the steeped mixture through a fine mesh sieve into a 1-cup measure, pressing down with a spoon to force through the liquid. If you have less than ⅓ cup liquid, add water to yield ⅓ cup.

Wash and rinse 4 or 5 (6- to 8-ounce) jelly jars, their metal screw rings, a ladle, and tongs in hot water. Place the jars and ladle in a large pot or canner of barely simmering water. Just before using, remove the jars with the tongs; drain upside down on toweling. Put the sealing lids into the simmering water for 2 minutes, then lay them underside up on the toweling.

Thoroughly stir together the remaining 2¼ cups water, the lemon juice, and pectin in a 6-quart or larger nonreactive pot or saucepan until smoothly blended. Bring to a full, rolling boil. Gradually stir in the sugar, then cook, stirring, until it dissolves and the jelly become clear. Stir in reserved lavender-infused

Tips: This recipe must be prepared with "classic" powdered pectin, not the newer low-sugar or no-sugar-needed pectin, nor the no-cooking-needed kind. I particularly recommend the "Original" or "Traditional" Sure-Jell brand of powdered fruit pectin for this recipe. The Sure-Jell version labeled for no- or low-sugar jams and jellies is *not* the product you want.

water. When the mixture returns to a full, rolling boil, boil exactly 2 minutes longer, stirring.

Immediately remove the pot from the heat. It will probably not look jelled; this takes several hours. Skim off and discard all foam. Ladle the jelly into the jars, leaving ½-inch headroom. Wipe any drips from jar rims and threads. Add the lids, then firmly screw on the rings. Put a rack or a folded tea towel in a large pot of simmering water. Lower the jars into the hot water bath; if they are not covered by 2 inches of water add more hot water. Cover the pot and bring the water to a gentle boil. Boil for 8 to 10 minutes. Remove the jars; set upright on a towel. Let cool completely. Check the jar seals by pressing down in the middle of the lids, if any spring back, the jars are not sealed. Store any unsealed jars in the refrigerator and use within a few weeks. Sealed jars may be kept in the pantry for up to a year. Makes about 4 cups jelly.

Peach-Orange Freezer Jam with Lavender

Freezer jams are quicker to make than regular jams—and some think they are also better. As you'll notice the moment you try this heavenly peach-orange version, they definitely come out tasting lighter and more like fresh, succulent, right-from-the-tree fruit. That's because they require less sugar and a shorter cooking time. Here, the natural appeal of ripe, summer peaches is cranked up even further with a little hit of lavender, ginger, and orange—oh my is this combo good!

The trade-off is that, as the name suggests, these jams are made a different way and **must** be stored in the freezer or refrigerator. And, you do still need to sterilize the jars and lids in boiling water before filling them with jam. Finally, you must use a pectin specifically labeled as suitable for reduced-sugar or no-sugar-needed jam recipes. Skip regular pectin, which requires a higher sugar content to set up, and "no cook" pectin, which is only for raw, uncooked preserves.

1½ to 2 tablespoons chopped fresh culinary lavender buds or dried culinary lavender buds

1¼ teaspoons **each** chopped peeled fresh gingerroot and freshly grated orange zest (orange part of the peel)

¾ cup boiling water

⅓ cup fresh lemon juice

2½ cups granulated sugar

3½ tablespoons lower- or no-sugar-needed pectin, such as Sure-Jell or Ball RealFruit Jell

3 cups chopped pitted peeled fresh ripe peaches (about 6 large)

1 cup fresh orange segments (free of all pith and membranes), chopped

Sterilize 5 (8-ounce) jelly jars, their screw-on rings, and a ladle in boiling water for 5 minutes. Drain upside down on paper towels to dry. Dip the jar lids in boiling water for 1 minute. Using tongs, lay them underside up on paper towels. Combine the lavender, gingerroot, and orange zest in a small, deep bowl. Pour the boiling water over them. Let stand to infuse for at least 15 minutes or up to 1 hour.

Strain the infused water through a very fine mesh sieve into a 1-cup measure, using a spoon to force through as much liquid as possible. If you have less than ⅔ cup, add enough water to yield ⅔ cup. Stir in the lemon juice. Set aside. Place several metal teaspoons in the refrigerator to use to check the jell of the jam.

With a long-handled spoon, thoroughly stir together the sugar and pectin in a 4-quart or larger wide-bottomed nonreactive pot until well blended and free of lumps. Stir in the lemon juice-infused water mixture, then the peaches and oranges until well blended. Cook over medium-high heat, stirring constantly, until the mixture comes to a **full, foaming boil**. Start timing and cook, stirring, for 2 minutes longer. Immediately drop a half teaspoon of hot jam onto a chilled spoon and let it cool for 30 seconds. If it runs off instead of jelling just slightly and clinging to the spoon, cook 1 minute longer, then check using another chilled spoon. As soon as the mixture just clings to the spoon and jells slightly, it is done. (It will continue to jell and thicken further upon cooling.) Immediately remove from the heat. Skim off and discard any foam from the surface. Let cool for 5 minutes.

Using the sterilized ladle, ladle the jam into the jars, leaving ¾-inch headroom to allow for expansion during freezing. Wipe any drips from the jar rim and threads, add the lids, then screw on the rings. Let stand until cooled to barely warm. Refrigerate for 24 hours. Check and tighten the lids if necessary. Freeze for up to 1 year, or refrigerate for up to 3 weeks. Makes 5 cups jam.

APPENDIX

||||||||||||||||||||||||||||||||||||||||||||||||||||||||||||||||||||||||||||||||||||||||||||||||||||||||

What Goes with Lavender: Affinities Pairing

Successfully creating delectable lavender dishes involves teaming up this highly aromatic herb with ingredients and flavors it just naturally goes with. The approach is sometimes called flavor affinities pairing, and many chefs, wine experts, and recipe developers, including me, swear by it when creating new dishes or menus. The idea is that when you combine compatible aroma and flavor elements, they automatically enhance and amplify one another, guaranteeing pleasing, even irresistible, results. One handy resource food professionals and creative home cooks use for guidance on what goes with what is *The Flavor Bible*, by Karen Page and Andrew Dornenburg. It features many hundreds of specific ingredients and pairing suggestions gathered from noted chefs. But perhaps because lavender is only now becoming widely known as a culinary ingredient, the book doesn't provide a huge amount of information about this herb.

I did find the book's listings a good starting point, then began experimenting and methodically taste-testing lavender paired with all kinds of ingredients and flavors to uncover as many other useful affinities as I could. It was instantly obvious that the herb is complex; in fact, lavender contains more than a hundred elements that can amplify, round out, and enhance other ingredients.

To give you just a glimpse into the complexity: A major component of culinary lavender, called *linalool*, has fragrance notes of lemon, orange, coriander, ginger, flowers, especially roses, stone fruits, berries, and sometimes mint. Lavender also has small amounts of *terpineol*, which has piney aromas reminiscent of rosemary and oregano, and *caryophyllene*, which has spicy notes reminiscent of cloves and black pepper. And these are only three of the **dozens** of compounds that contribute to lavender's flavor profile! (Remember that because our taste buds only detect sweet, sour, salty, bitter, and umami, much of what we "taste" actually involves the aromas we inhale as we eat.)

Following are the current results of my taste tests. First, you'll see sets of ingredients containing lavender that I've found always taste wonderful together. In each grouping the ingredients are synergistic—they not only deliver extraordinarily tempting (sometimes completely novel) results but they taste significantly better in concert than when sampled individually. I've followed up with lists of single ingredients that pair well with lavender; the bolded items have a particularly strong affinity for it. I know there are still many more affinities to be discovered, but these will help get you off to a good start.

STRONG SYNERGISTIC AFFINITIES FORMULATIONS

lavender + oranges (or apricots) + honey + ground coriander

lavender + peaches (or nectarines)+ fresh ginger

lavender + cooked tomatoes + oregano + thyme

lavender + soy sauce + fresh ginger + allspice + brown sugar

lavender + vanilla + pomegranate juice + honey

lavender + pecans + orange + allspice + sugar

lavender + lime (or lemon) + fresh ginger + ginger ale

lavender + cream + honey + vanilla

lavender + apples + apple juice + fresh or smoked pork + thyme

lavender + black and white pepper + pink peppercorns

lavender + curry powder + allspice + thyme + raisins (or sweetened cranberries)

lavender + allspice + cinnamon + nutmeg + ground ginger + sugar

lavender + blackberries + fresh lemon (or lime) zest

lavender + lamb + rosemary + thyme

lavender + plums + vanilla + honey

lavender + chocolate + raspberries or blackberries

lavender + pears (or apples) + fresh ginger + vanilla + honey

lavender + white beans + sun-dried tomatoes + oregano

lavender + salmon + soy sauce + honey + fresh ginger

lavender + fresh tomatoes + balsamic vinegar + olive oil + black pepper

lavender + smoked meat + brown sugar or maple syrup

lavender + peaches + oranges + honey + mild, creamy cheese

INGREDIENTS LAVENDER GOES WITH (bolded items have a strong affinity)

Herbs
basil
chamomile
chives
cilantro
cumin
dill weed
garlic
marjoram
mint
oregano
parsley
rosemary
sage
tarragon
thyme
winter savory

Spices
allspice
anise
black pepper
cardamom
caraway
cayenne pepper
cinnamon
cloves
coriander
curry powder
fennel seed
ginger
nutmeg
mace
mustard seed
pink peppercorn
saffron

Fruits
apples
apricots
blackberries
blueberries
blood oranges
cantaloupe
cherries
coconut
cranberries
dates
figs
grapes
grapefruit
honeydew melon
kumquats
lemons
limes
mandarin oranges
oranges
peaches
pears
pineapple
pomegranate
passion fruit
plums
raisins
raspberries
strawberries
tangerines
watermelon

Meats, Poultry, Seafood
bacon
beef
chicken
duck
ham
lamb
pork
rabbit
sausage
salmon
shrimp
smoked meats
smoked fish
turkey
venison

Vegetables, Beans and Starches
beets
carrots
chick peas
corn
fennel
lentils
mushrooms
onions
parsnips
potatoes
pumpkin
rice
sweet potatoes
tomatoes
white beans
winter squash

Condiments, Sauces, Extracts
barbeque sauce
balsamic vinegar
caramel sauce
chocolate sauce
fruit chutney
fruit jams
honey
hot sauce
ketchup
maple syrup
mayonnaise
molasses
mustard
rose water
soy sauce
sweet and sour sauce
vanilla

Dairy Products
brie
buratta
butter
camembert
cream
cream cheese
fontina
havarti
ice cream
marscapone
monterey jack
mozzarella
ricotta

Nuts
almonds,
cashews
hazelnuts
pecans
peanuts
pistachios
walnuts

Miscellaneous
bread
bread stuffing
brown sugar
cakes
cookies
chocolate
cornbread
cocoa powder
custards
olive oil
pasta
peanut oil
scones
shortbread
sugar
white chocolate

Beverages
apple juice
apple cider
apple brandy
chai tea
cream sherry
crème de cassis
grape juice
herb tea
orange juice
orange liqueurs
pineapple juice
ginger ale
kirsch
lemonade
limeade
marsala
moscato
peach schnapps
pomegranate juice
port
prosecco
Riesling
tea

LAVENDER RESOURCES

While a variety of gourmet shops around the country carry lavender, my comprehensive list of lavender farms and herb shops that sell culinary lavender offers you many more local and regional options: Go to www.nancyslavenderplace.com and click on Resources. My site also provides more exclusive lavender recipes; beautiful photos of lavender and lavender farms; tips on buying and cooking with lavender; and much more. Information on and reviews of the book are available and additional copies of *The Art of Cooking with Lavender* can be purchased there as well.

Here are some of my other useful lavender-related posts, videos, and photos available online:

www.youtube.com/user/nancybaggettvideos
www.facebook.com/NancysLavenderPlace/
https://twitter.com/nancybaggett
www.instagram.com/nancy_baggett/
www.pinterest.com/nancybaggett/
www.kitchenlane.com

The U.S. Lavender Growers Association lists member lavender farms that sell lavender on-line and/or in their shops and provides hotlinks to members' websites. The USLGA website also provides Information on lavender events and festivals and how to get started growing lavender. Go to: http://uslavender.org/resources/member-products-and-services-directory/ For basic Lavender 101 information go to: http://uslavender.org/category/lavender-101/

HIGHLY RECOMMENDED BOOKS ON LAVENDER

Bader, Sarah Berringer, 2012, *The Lavender Lover's Handbook*, Portland, Oregon: Timber Press—

Approachable, beautiful, and inspiring, Sarah Bader's book offers the lavender fan a wealth of information and photographs on lavender varieties, plus helpful details on growing, crafting, and getting started cooking with lavender.

Upson, Tim, and Andrews, Susyn 2004, *The Genus Lavandula*, Portland, Oregon: Timber Press—

A 400-page comprehensive and authoritative illustrated reference work for the serious lavender enthusiast, *The Genus Lavandula* covers history, cultivation, commercial use and taxonomy of 39 species and nearly 400 cultivars of lavender.

INDEX

Acknowledgements

I'm grateful to well-known herb expert and my long-time culinary friend, Susan Belsinger, for reviewing my manuscript and suggesting changes and corrections. It is a more accurate book as a result of her sharp eye and key input. I'm also grateful to my U.S. Lavender Growers Association colleague, Mesha Munyan, of Meshaz Natural Perfumes, for her demonstration of lavender distillation and some informal "nose" training.

A thank you also goes to the many North American lavender farmers whose beautiful lavender fields and gardens and top-quality culinary lavender products have inspired me. I am particularly grateful to my colleagues in the U.S. Lavender Growers Association for providing helpful information and for being enthusiastic supporters of this book project. And a huge thanks to all those who have allowed me and my husband, and, on several occasions, my grandchildren (shown above) to visit to explore, learn, photograph, and enjoy your beautiful lavender farms:

B & B Family Farm, 5883 Old Olympic Hwy, Sequim, WA 98382 www.bbfamilyfarm.com
Deep Creek Lavender Farm, 625 Doerr Rd, Accident, MD 21520 www.deepcreeklavenderfarm.com
Fat Cat Garden & Gifts, 21 Fat Cat Lane Sequim, WA 98382 www.fatcat-lavender.com
Graysmarsh Berry Farm, 6187 Woodcock Rd, Sequim, WA 98382 www.graysmarsh.com
Le Jardin du Soleil, 3932 Sequim Dungeness Way, Sequim, WA www.jardindusoleil.com
Lavender Wind Farm, 2530 Darst Rd., Coupeville, WA 98239 www.lavenderwind.com
Martha Lane Lavender Farm, 371 Martha Ln, Sequim, WA 98382 www.marthalanelavender.com
Olympic Lavender, 120 W Washington St, Sequim WA 98382 www.olympiclavender.com
Purple Haze Lavender Farm, 180 Bell Bottom Rd, Sequim, WA 98382 www.purplehazelavender.com
The Lavender Connection, 1141 Cays Rd, Sequim, WA 98382 www.lavenderconnection.com
Victor's Lavender, 3743 Old Olympic Hwy, Port Angeles, WA 98362 www.victorslavender.com
Washington Lavender Farm, 65 Finn Hall Rd, Port Angeles, WA 98362 www.walavender.com
Woodinville Lavender, 14223 Woodinville-Redmond Rd NE, Redmond, WA 98052
www.woodinvillelavender.com

Thanks, too, to the talented, hard-working professionals involved in producing this book: Designer Chrissy Kurpeski, who created the beautiful cover and interior design; production artist Patty Holden, who worked tirelessly to ready the book for printing; and to copy editor, Deri Reed, who helped smooth and improve the text. Finally, as always, thanks to my family, my biggest supporters and fans!

ABOUT THE AUTHOR

Nancy Baggett is an award-winning cookbook author, food journalist, hobbyist gardener, and food photographer with nearly twenty books and hundreds of articles to her credit. Her cookbooks include *The International Chocolate Cookbook*, an International Association of Culinary Professionals (IACP) Best Baking Book winner, and her very popular *The All American Cookie Book*, which was both a James Beard Foundation and IACP cookbook award nominee. Her articles have appeared in numerous well-known publications, including *Better Homes and Gardens*, *Country Gardens*, *Bon Appetit*, *Food & Wine*, *Eating Well*, and *The Washington Post*. She also has dozens of stories, photos, recipes, and cooking videos on her website, www.kitchenlane.com, and lots of lavender-related information, resources, and photography on her new website, www.nancyslavenderplace.com

Nancy became interested in growing and cooking with lavender after discovering the great power of the more familiar culinary herbs to tempt the taste buds and brighten dull dishes. She spied some pots of lavender in bloom at a garden center, and it was love at first sight! Lavender's incredible fragrance and beauty bowled her over, and she has been smitten with it ever since. She started adding lavender to baked goods and sweets—with delectable results—then later began exploring the many ways it can also enhance savory dishes. She created *The Art of Cooking with Lavender* after several years of kitchen exploration and many visits to lavender farms to learn and take photographs. The book recently won a "Books for Better Living," award from Independent Publisher and has garnered praise from many readers and cooks. Nancy grows about forty lavender plants, mostly culinary varies, and delights in harvesting them each summer and cooking with them throughout the year.

Nancy has been a guest chef on hundreds of television and radio shows around the country, including *Good Morning America*, and NPR's *All Things Considered*. You can check out clips of appearances, plus some how-to videos on her youtube channel, listed below. She is active on a variety of social media platforms, regularly posting photos, videos, recipes, and cooking and lavender information. You may want to start with www.nancyslavenderplace.com , but will also find interesting lavender posts on the other links listed here.

www.youtube.com/user/nancybaggettvideos
www.facebook.com/NancysLavenderPlace/
https://twitter.com/nancybaggett
www.instagram.com/nancy_baggett/
www.pinterest.com/nancybaggett/
www.kitchenlane.com